WRITERS AND THEIR WORK

ISOBEL ARMSTRONG
General Editor

JOSEPH CONRAD

JOSEPH CONRAD

from a dry-point by WALTER TITTLE *by courtesy of the Trustees of The National Portrait Gallery*

JOSEPH CONRAD

Cedric Watts

NORTHCOTE

BRITISH COUNCIL

ATLANTIC
PUBLISHERS & DISTRIBUTORS (P) LTD

This edition is published by

ATLANTIC

PUBLISHERS & DISTRIBUTORS (P) LTD

7/22, Ansari Road, Darya Ganj, New Delhi-110 002
Tel: 40775252, 23273880, 23275880, 23280451; Fax: +91-11-23285873
E-mail: orders@atlanticbooks.com; Web: www.atlanticbooks.com

By arrangement with
Northcote House Publishers Ltd
Horndon House, Horndon, Tavistock, Devon, PL19 9NQ,
United Kingdom. (T)+44(0)1822 810066; (F)+44(0)1822 810034
(E) northcote.house@virgin.net and (W) www.northcotehouse.co.uk
The *Writers and their Work* series is published in association with the British Council.

First Indian Reprint 2010
First published in 1994 by Northcote House Publishers Ltd

ISBN 978-81-269-1307-7

British Library Cataloguing-in-Publication Data
A catalogue record for this book is available from the British Library

Typeset by Kestrel Data, Exeter
Printed in India at Nice Printing Press, A-33/3A, Site-IV,
Industrial Area, Sahibabad, Ghaziabad, U.P.

Contents

Preface

The publishers specify that works in this series should be short (between 15,000 and 25,000 words) and should aim for clarity of exposition. I have endeavoured, within this concise format, to give some indications of the range, richness and diversity of Joseph Conrad's literary output. The 'story' told here is of Conrad's arduous route from his Polish origins to his eventual success, in both critical and financial terms, as a creative writer in English. I note various paradoxes and ironies, not only within Conrad's works, but also in his reception. For example, the very experimentalism which alienated many of his early reviewers won him subsequent critical acclaim. In the period 1945–75, his reputation reached new heights as the 'difficult' texts, 'Heart of Darkness', *Lord Jim* and *Nostromo* moved into the foreground of discussion. In more recent years, various feminists, left-wing critics and 'postcolonial' writers have challenged his eminence. The tensions and divisions within his works make it likely that he will long remain a focus of lively debate. I hope that the reader will complement the glimpses and hints offered within the short scope of this book by using some of the materials listed in the Bibliography, and, above all, by reading Conrad.

Note on the Text

In this study, quotations from Conrad's literary works are taken from the 'Collected Edition' published by J. M. Dent & Sons (London, 1946–55).

Biographical Outline

Józef Teodor Konrad Nałęcz Korzeniowski was born on 3 December 1857 in the Russian-controlled area of Poland. In 1861 his patriotic parents were arrested and in 1862 sent into exile; his father died in 1865, his mother in 1869. In 1874 Conrad left Poland for the south of France to become a seaman. After service in French vessels (and a suicide attempt when in debt), he travelled to England and joined the Merchant Navy, rising to the rank of captain and serving in a variety of ships between 1878 and 1894. He took British nationality in 1886. Ten years later he married Jessie George; his sons, Borys and John, were born in 1898 and 1906 respectively.

His main fictional works are: *Almayer's Folly* (1895); *An Outcast of the Islands* (1896); *The Nigger of the 'Narcissus'* (serial and book, 1897); *Tales of Unrest* (including 'An Outpost of Progress', 1898); 'Heart of Darkness' (serial, 1899); *Lord Jim* (serial, 1899–1900; book, 1900), *Youth* (including 'Heart of Darkness', 1902); *Typhoon* (serials and book, 1902); *Nostromo* (serial and book, 1904); *The Secret Agent* (serial, 1906–7; book, 1907); *A Set of Six* (1908); *Under Western Eyes* (serials, 1910–11; book, 1911); *'Twixt Land and Sea* (1912); *Chance* (serial, 1912; book, 1914); *Within the Tides* (1915); *Victory* (serials and book, 1915); *The Shadow-Line* (serials, 1916–17; book, 1917); *The Arrow of Gold* (serial, 1918–20; book, 1919); *The Rescue* (serials, 1919–20; book, 1920); *The Rover* (serial and book, 1923); *Tales of Hearsay* (1925); and *Suspense* (unfinished; serials and book, 1925). He adapted as plays *The Secret Agent*, 'Because of the Dollars' (dramatized as *Laughing Anne*) and 'To-morrow' (as *One Day More*). With Ford Madox Hueffer he collaborated in writing *The Inheritors* (1901), *Romance* (1903) and 'The Nature of a Crime' (1909).

His main non-fictional works are: *The Mirror of the Sea* (aided by Hueffer, 1906); *A Personal Record* (1912); *Notes on Life and Letters* (1921); and *Last Essays* (1926).

Though his writings often won high praise from reviewers, during many years of his literary career he struggled with increasing financial debts. He was sustained largely by loans from his faithful literary agent, J. B. Pinker. In 1914, however, Conrad became a popular and lucrative author, acclaimed in the United States as well as in Great Britain. He declined numerous honorary degrees and a knighthood. Conrad died on 3 August 1924 and was buried at Canterbury.

1

Homo Duplex

Joseph Conrad: Polish nobleman and British citizen; master mariner and dedicated author; moralist and sceptic; traditionalist and modernist; reserved and fervent; pessimistic and humane. Aptly, he called himself '*homo duplex*', the double man. He can be seen as one of the most paradoxical of literary figures: his art, at its most interesting and intense, constantly aspires to the condition of paradox. We find eloquent warnings against eloquence; linguistic virtuosity and a sense of the inadequacy of language; a commitment to solidarity and a preoccupation with isolation; traditional moral affirmations and radically sceptical insights; philosophical sophistication and a fear that reflection paralyses the will; atheistic assumptions and supernatural implications; romantic enthusiasms and cynical ironies; hostility to revolutionaries yet sympathy for rebels. His works have been termed 'janiform', for any tutelary deity of theirs may be the god Janus: the two-faced god who looks in opposite directions at the same time.

In Conrad's early and major phases as a writer from 1895 to 1911, his work was, arguably, more radical than that of any contemporaneous novelist. In matters political, cultural, psychological and linguistic, Conrad was outstanding in his ability to search, test and question. His scepticism was an acid that burnt deeply into the ideological alloys of his age, yet his sense of humanity and beauty endured to preserve him from facile endorsements of absurdity and nihilism. He challenged the assumptions of civilization; but, from the totality of his novels, tales, essays and letters, emerges the model of an admirably civilized self: Olympian yet sensitive, intelligent yet modest, responsive to the past yet vigilant to the future. The more critically he weighed nineteenth-century preoccupations, the more fully he anticipated twentieth-century preoccupations: notably, the modern concerns with linguistic ambiguity, with economic and cultural imperialism, with irrationality in the self and the world, and with the problem of moral affirmation in a sceptical era. Virtually from birth, he had been initiated into the problematic.

In 1857 Józef Teodor Konrad Nałęcz Korzeniowski (later to be known as Joseph Conrad) was born into a Poland which had practically vanished from the map of Europe. In a series of 'partitions' at the end of the eighteenth century, the country had been annexed by Russia from the east, Prussia from the west, and Austria from the south. Conrad was brought up in the part of Poland which was controlled by the Russians. His parents, patriotic members of the *szlachta* (the land-owning gentry-cum-nobility), conspired against the Russian overlords, were arrested, found guilty of subversive activities, and exiled to the remote province of Vologda; the 4-year-old son accompanied them into exile. Partly as a result of their privations, both parents died young, leaving Conrad an orphan at the age of 11. So Conrad had gained early and bitter experience of the force of imperialism, of the paradox that loyalty to one cause may resemble treachery to another, and of the inter-connection of solidarity with isolation; the apparent sanctuary may be the site of ambush, and ideals may be fatal illusions. All these themes were to characterize his eventual literary texts.

When he was 16, he left Poland for France, worked among the seamen of Marseille, voyaged to the West Indies in French ships, lucklessly gambled with borrowed money at Monte Carlo, and narrowly survived a suicide attempt: he shot himself in the chest, but the bullet missed his heart. In 1878 he entered the British Merchant Navy, and during the next sixteen years made many voyages on sailing-ships and steamships, qualifying as second mate, first mate and eventually as captain. He became a British citizen in 1886 (renouncing Russian citizenship) and made London his base between those voyages which took him to Bombay, Singapore, the East Indies, Australia and the Congo Free State. In Poland he had shared the life of a nation subjected to (though not vanquished by) imperialism; but in England he shared the life of a nation at the height of her imperial power, dominating the greatest empire the world had known. He could respond to the glamour, the moral assumptions, the Titanism and romantic hubris of the endeavour, even while his shrewd scepticism and his patrician distaste for commercialism alerted him to its hypocrisies and myopia. As Marlow was to say in 'Heart of Darkness':

> The conquest of the earth, which mostly means the taking it away from those who have a different complexion or slightly flatter noses than ourselves, is not a pretty thing when you look into it too much.

Like many other Poles, Conrad was an Anglophile, regarding Britain as a land which reconciled tradition, stability, and respect for individual liberties. Internationally in the Victorian age, British administrators, officers, explorers and travellers often wielded a distinct prestige, as did the image of 'the English gentleman' – reticent, honourable, firm, keen on 'fair play'. It was an image which often masked the extremely unfair reality of colonialism. From the pen of an American visitor, Henry James, flowed heightened imitations (in style and characterization) of 'the sophisticated European'; and in the pages of the Polish-born Conrad, 'the British officer and gentleman' were to find observant, partly critical, partly flattering reflection. (Instances include Charles Marlow, Charles Gould, Captain Brierly, 'Lord' Jim, and the anonymous captains in 'The Secret Sharer' and *The Shadow-Line*.) On his voyages, Conrad served the traditions of the Merchant Navy, and his vessels' cargoes helped to sustain the trade of the empire – coal from Newcastle to Bangkok, wool and wheat from Sydney to London. While crossing the oceans, he accumulated an abundance of experience to supply his later novels: exotic landscapes and seascapes; storm and calm; tropical shores; a diversity of characters of different nations, known or merely glimpsed. Seamanship provided an ethical code which depended not on metaphysical postulates but on the practicalities of survival. He recognized the ship as political microcosm, a floating community, but also experienced the littleness of a humanity encompassed by the immensity of sea and sky, beneath the cold serenity of the stars and the infinity of space. And, at landfall, in Java or Sumatra or Borneo, the encounter with the indigenous peoples could provoke a questioning of European assumptions. What were the bases of civilization and what was the real nature of 'progress'? Were there any essential differences between the Europeans and those they sought to colonize? The heroine of his first novel, *Almayer's Folly*, would reflect bitterly that 'there was no change and no difference'; and Stein in *Lord Jim* would declare:

> Man is amazing, but he is not a masterpiece [. . .] Perhaps the artist was a little mad [. . .] Sometimes it seems to me that man is come where he is not wanted, where there is no place for him; for if not, why should he

> want all the place? Why should he run about here and there making a great noise about himself, talking about the stars, disturbing the blades of grass?

In *Last Essays,* Conrad bluntly termed imperialism in Africa 'the vilest scramble for loot that ever disfigured the history of human conscience'.

As he travelled among different nations and races, Conrad travelled through different linguistic terrains. He was linguistically inquisitive and acquisitive, experiencing words as lenses and veils, as revelatory and duplicitous. While his native language was Polish, he had lived in a region where the peasants spoke Ukrainian and the overlords Russian. His father, who introduced him to the patriotic works of Adam Mickiewicz, was a translator of English and French texts (by Shakespeare, Alfred de Vigny and Victor Hugo). Conrad's own second language was French: the courtly French of civilized address, the lucid literary French of Flaubert, Maupassant and Anatole France, and the vernacular of Mediterranean seamen. His English was acquired partly from his voracious reading (of Shakespeare, Byron, Dickens, Carlyle and many others) and partly from fellow sailors. 'My teachers', he claimed, 'had been the sailors of the Norfolk shore; coast men, with steady eyes, mighty limbs, and gentle voice; men of very few words, which at least were never bare of meaning.'

Conrad had needed one kind of courage when he persevered in his maritime career: courage to face the ordeals and perils of arduous voyages, at a time when deaths by shipwreck were an everyday occurrence. He needed courage of another kind when he embarked on his second career, as a professional novelist; for he was working ambitiously in a foreign language. 'I had to work like a coal miner in his pit quarrying all my English sentences out of a black night', he recalled. He possessed cultural ideals, yet a strong sense of cultural relativism; literary ambitions, yet a strong sense of linguistic entropy. Different languages smuggled different assumptions; and, if English was becoming an international currency, it was a currency that could become debased and devalued: 'The old, old words, worn thin, defaced'. He knew that clichés of phrase were also clichés of thought and feeling, and he assailed them in texts which were exuberant in their range of linguistic resource. For him, language was the medium of conjuration. It evoked, summoned and co-ordinated an imagined world; it could recall, transform and exorcise too, reconciling the diversities of his experience and laying to rest the ghosts of the past and the hauntings of guilt. Some Poles saw Conrad as a renegade – as one who had deserted his beleaguered nation and chosen to write in another tongue; and his works repeatedly display real or imagined treacheries, sometimes punished, sometimes vindicated. In *A Personal Record,* he wrote:

> It would take too long to explain the intimate alliance of contradictions in human nature which makes love itself wear at times the desperate shape of betrayal.

The young Conrad had gambled and lost at Monte Carlo. In the early 1890s it must sometimes have seemed to him that he had gambled and lost as a seaman. As steam gradually superseded sail, and as ships became larger and more efficient, fewer officers were needed: it had become harder for him to find appointments that matched his qualifications. In abandoning the sea for a writer's career, he was gambling again. The odds against him, however, were reduced by various cultural and economic factors which made the 1890s a Golden Age for aspiring writers. The enormous expansion of education in Victorian Britain (to harness the democratic electorate) had created a vast literate public, and technological advances had reduced the costs of newsprint, books and magazines. To supply the needs of an increasing readership, publishing houses multiplied and expanded, while a diversity of periodicals flourished. The market was strengthened by municipal public libraries, commercial circulating libraries such as Smith's and Mudie's, subscription libraries like the London Library (which Conrad himself would join in 1897), and clubs like the Athenaeum and Junior Carlton (where John Galsworthy would see fellow members requesting fiction by Conrad). Many magazines published tales and serialized novels; many more gave abundant space to reviews of current literary works; and there was even a *Review of Reviews*. Never before, and seldom subsequently, could British-based novelists enjoy opportunities as great as those provided in the 1890s. The Chace Act of 1891 ensured that authors could receive payment if their books were republished in the United States. Indeed, Conrad would frequently be paid several times for the same piece of work: for British and American serialization, for the British and American book editions, for continental publication in English (as in the Tauchnitz series, Leipzig) or in translation; a text might be adapted for the theatre (as *The Secret Agent* and *Victory* would be); and eventually, of course, there might be the accolade of a collected edition. Magazine payments were often remarkably generous: in 1897, for instance, *Blackwood's Magazine* sent Conrad £40 for the tale 'Karain' – more than half the annual earnings of a bricklayer and twice the amount that Conrad's maid would earn by a year's work in 1900.

The market variously influenced Conrad's output. The large number of his short works can be explained partly by the receptivity of magazines to tales and essays. Some of his novels were written with particular periodicals in mind, and *The Nigger of the 'Narcissus'* was enduringly inflected as a result. Sometimes Conrad aimed his work at a discerning readership and an appreciative posterity; at other times, seeking popularity or easy payment, he produced relatively trivial items. Both his best and his worst work appeared in periodicals: even the complex masterpiece, *Nostromo,* was first published in *T. P.'s Weekly,* so that Conrad's indictment of 'material interests' accompanied advertisements for 'Magnetic Healing', 'Scrubb's Preparation' (which cleans hair, carpets and cutlery) and 'Patent Nose Machines' (to 'improve ugly noses of all kinds'). Individual works thus become diversified: the serial version of *Nostromo* contains important material lacking in the subsequent book.

Though Joseph Conrad would endure many years of financial struggles before eventually prospering as a writer, his debts were largely a consequence of his prodigality in expenditure and his slow rate of production, not of any lack of opportunity and reward. When Conrad had become an orphan and later pursued his career at sea, he repeatedly received financial help from his wealthy uncle, Tadeusz Bobrowski. The knowledge that Bobrowski would bequeath him a substantial sum (in the event, £1,600, received in 1895) facilitated Conrad's change of career. Since Bobrowski was a land-owner, whose income derived largely from the rents paid by tenant-farmers, a financial conduit had linked Conrad to the distant tillers of the Polish soil. During the struggles of his literary career, Conrad was sustained by numerous figures. Some of his publishers (notably William Blackwood, who serialized 'Youth', 'Heart of Darkness' and *Lord Jim*) were generously considerate. Various friends, including Ford Madox Hueffer and John Galsworthy, provided loans. The British taxpayer furnished a 'Civil List' pension and other subsidies. Crucially, James Brand Pinker, Conrad's agent from

1900 until 1922, risked thousands of pounds (a vast amount in today's equivalents) by supporting the author in the belief that his writings would eventually become lucrative. Nevertheless, had Conrad foreseen the decades of debt, depression and gnawing self-doubt which lay ahead, it is by no means certain that he would have embarked on his literary career. In 1894, however, he wrapped the manuscript of *Almayer's Folly* in two pieces of cardboard and some brown paper, enclosed twelve penny stamps in case of rejection, and sent it to the publishing house of T. Fisher Unwin.

2

Early Writings

T. Fisher Unwin accepted *Almayer's Folly* for publication on the advice of two of his 'readers' (assessors of manuscripts): W. H. Chesson and Edward Garnett. 'The magical melancholy of that masterpiece submerged me', Chesson alliteratively recalled. While Chesson arranged publicity for the book, Edward Garnett introduced himself to Conrad and became, for many years, a 'literary midwife' to the struggling author, whom he helped with detailed advice and sympathetically perceptive reviews. He was Conrad's most loyal and intelligent publicist. Other writers whose careers were established largely by Garnett's endeavours were to include John Galsworthy, W. H. Hudson, R. B. Cunninghame Graham, W. H. Davies, D. H. Lawrence, Dorothy Richardson, T. E. Lawrence, H. E. Bates and Henry Green. The cultural significance of publishers' readers like Chesson and Garnett has long been underestimated. Reviewers and academic critics appraise works which are *already* in print, but the publishers' readers decide which new manuscripts are worthy of being preserved in type instead of being consigned to oblivion.

Fisher Unwin, politically a Liberal, acquired the reputation of being a rather cold, calculating, tightfisted publisher; *The Inheritors*, written by Conrad and Hueffer, would depict him as the miserly Polehampton. In fairness, it should be noted that he not only was prompt to publish *Almayer's Folly*, but also met the author personally, encouraged him to maintain his literary ambitions, provided remarkably extensive publicity, and entered into a detailed postal discussion of Conrad's literary plans. 'He has *means* to push a book – the connection and the best agent in the trade', the author noted. Conrad, temperamentally prickly yet depressively self-doubting, needed such encouragement even more than would most novitiates.

On 25 April 1895, four days before publication of *Almayer's Folly*, favourable publicity (evidently arranged by Chesson) appeared in the Liberal *Daily News*:

> No novelist has yet annexed the island of Borneo – in itself almost a continent. But Mr. Joseph Conrad, a new writer, is about to make the attempt in a novel entitled *Almayer's Folly*, which Mr. Unwin will publish. Mr. Conrad says that he combines 'the psychological study of a sensitive European living alone among semi-hostile Arabs and Malays with the vivid incidents attaching to the life of pirates and smugglers.' A merely 'sensitive' European has no business among the semi-savages of Borneo. What you want is an unbounded, reckless hospitality to all sorts of impressions. However the story is praised by those who have seen it in manuscript. The author is intimately acquainted with Borneo and its people. The physical setting of his story is as picturesque as the world offers. The European's closest friend is an ex-pirate, and the reassertion of the old savage instinct in the pirate's lovely daughter – an atavistic fit, if that be not too rude an expression – is one of the chief incidents of the tale.

This 'kite' or 'trailer' for the book is a good instance of the marketing tactics of that era. The paragraph opens with a candid acknowledgement of the connection between political and literary imperialism: a new act of annexation is to take place – this time, the literary annexation of Borneo by Conrad (following that of India by Kipling and of the South Seas by Stevenson). The statement attributed to Conrad shrewdly appeals both to intellectuals ('the psychological study of a sensitive European') and to readers seeking a lively yarn ('vivid incidents [. . .] pirates and smugglers'). The columnist's reservation ('What you want is an unbounded, reckless hospitality to all sorts of impressions') may perhaps have encouraged Conrad to envisage the more kaleidoscopic methods of *Lord Jim* and *Nostromo*, methods which some subsequent critics were to term 'literary impressionism'. As for the paragraph's final remark on 'the reassertion of the old savage instinct in the pirate's lovely daughter' (which confuses Nina Almayer with Lingard's protégée): this perhaps offers a blandishment to readers hoping for titillation coupled with some post-Darwinian drama of degeneration.

Most of the features specified in this publicity-notice can certainly be found in *Almayer's Folly*. A remarkable aspect of many of Conrad's novels and tales is that, when briefly summarized, they seem to belong to the realm of popular commercial fiction. *Almayer's Folly* does indeed tell of piracy, smuggling, shipwreck, exotic races, strife in the jungle, and the elopement of a beautiful Eurasian with a Balinese warrior-prince. But Conrad made adventure introspective, heroism ambiguous, the exotic subversive; he liked to question stereotypical contrasts between the 'civilized' and the 'primitive'; and dominant themes in the novel include the psychological isolation of individuals, the disparity between the ideal and the real, and the littleness of humanity before the inhuman vastness of nature. He transmuted the elements of romantic melodrama into the ambiguities of philosophical tragedy. By a variety of descriptive and narrative devices, he subverted orthodox narration and magnified the thematic and ideological matter.

While Conrad preserved a strong sense of absurdity and satire, his temperamental pessimism had been amply reinforced by his study of Arthur Schopenhauer's dismal philosophy, by the sceptical fiction of Turgenev, Flaubert, Maupassant and Anatole France, by his knowledge of the Second Law of Thermodynamics (which implied that the sun must cool and all the earth's life become extinct), and by his post-Darwinian awareness of 'nature, red in tooth and claw'. Compared with such leading contemporaneous writers as Rider Haggard, Robert Louis Stevenson and Rudyard Kipling, Conrad was, in the largest sense, anti-imperialistic, for he repeatedly suggested that all human endeavours were doomed to defeat by the greater environment in which human awareness was an anomaly. Sometimes this environmental pessimism was so emphatic as to invite parody (and Max Beerbohm later accepted the invitation). Here, for example:

> As he skirted in his weary march the edge of the forest he glanced now and then into its dark shade, so enticing in its deceptive appearance of coolness, so repellent with its unrelieved gloom, where lay, entombed and rotting, countless generations of trees, and where their successors stood as if in mourning, in dark green foliage, immense and helpless, awaiting their turn. Only the parasites seemed to live there [. . .]

This first novel is in some ways cumbrous and laboured, with its long retrospects and strenuously wrought (sometimes over-wrought) descriptive set-pieces: it lacks the incisive verve and spectacular mobility of his mature works. Yet it remains formidable in its sombre ironies, its philosophical and political pessimism, in its modulations from lyrical melancholy to macabre black comedy, and in its justified obliquities in narrative technique. One of those obliquities is the use of 'delayed decoding', whereby the reader is presented with an effect but is denied (for a considerable interval) its cause, explanation or true interpretation. (For example, the reader is obliged to share, for many pages, Almayer's erroneous belief that a corpse found at the riverside is that of his friend Dain.) A related obliquity is the use of the 'covert plot': a plot-sequence so elliptically presented that it is unlikely to be grasped as a whole until a second or subsequent reading of the novel. The main covert plot of *Almayer's Folly* is Abdulla's scheme to destroy Almayer, his trade rival, by betraying Dain to the Dutch authorities. As a consequence of the betrayal, Dain's elopement to Bali with Nina Almayer is precipitated, Almayer's hopes of finding gold and returning to Europe with his beloved daughter are dashed, and Almayer's death as an opium-addict ensues. Appropriately, the novel ends with a sanctimonious invocation (of 'Allah! The Merciful! The Compassionate!') uttered by Abdulla over the body of 'this Infidel he had fought so long and had bested so many times'. What renders Abdulla's scheme covert is that for most of the time the reader shares the viewpoint of Almayer, the largely uncomprehending victim; so that only a careful subsequent reading makes clear the extent of Abdulla's involvement. Similarly, although the novel has some recourse to racial stereotypes, not until a second reading may one fully appreciate the extent to which those stereotypical contrasts have been questioned by the sceptical emphasis on common features: dreams of power and wealth, it seems, make all races kin. In his 'Author's Note' to the novel, Conrad declared:

> I am content to sympathize with common mortals, no matter where they live; in houses or in tents, in the streets under a fog, or in the forests behind the dark line of dismal mangroves that fringe the vast solitude of the sea. For, their land – like ours – lies under the inscrutable eyes of the Most High. Their hearts – like ours – must endure the load of the gifts from Heaven: the curse of facts and the blessing of illusions, the bitterness of our wisdom and the deceptive consolation of our folly.

The crux of *Almayer's Folly* is markedly anti-racist. For a while, Almayer is tempted to abandon his racial prejudice and accompany Nina and Dain to their new life in Bali; but his pride, vanity and self-pity destructively prevail.

On the novel's appearance, the *World* declared it 'wearisome' and 'dull', while the *Nation* (USA) remarked: 'Borneo is a fine field for the study of monkeys, not men'. Other complaints were that the story was 'hard to follow': 'The action drags' (*Bookman*). The dominant emphasis, however, was on the emergence of a distinctive and powerful new writer. The *Scotsman* found the novel 'remarkable' and 'powerfully imagined'; the *Daily Chronicle* said: 'Mr. Conrad has [. . .] the art of creating an atmosphere, poetic, romantic [. . .] Mr. Conrad may go on, and with confidence; he will find his public, and he deserves his place'; and the *Athenaeum*, while regretting the stylistic 'convolutions', emphasized the book's promise: 'We shall await with interest Mr. Conrad's next appearance as a novelist.' H. G. Wells in the *Saturday Review* said: 'It is indeed exceedingly well imagined and well written, and will secure Mr. Conrad a high place among contemporary story-tellers.' The *Speaker, Literary News* and the *Spectator* added their praise, the last remarking: 'The name of Mr. Joseph Conrad is new to us, but it appears to us as if he might become the Kipling of the Malay Archipelago.' In the *Weekly Sun*, the editor (T. P. O'Connor, who was later to serialize *Nostromo* in *T. P.'s Weekly*) devoted the whole front page to this 'startling, unique, splendid book'. On the whole, then, a body of reviews to provide Conrad not only with gratification but also with strong encouragement to become a full-time fiction-writer.

Meanwhile, Conrad proceeded with *An Outcast of the Islands*, continuing the Lingard Saga, the story of the establishment, decline and fall of Tom Lingard's trading empire – an ironic epic which cast sombre reflections on imperialism as a whole. By a process of imagination that was entirely characteristic, Conrad reversed chronological order: the final stage of the saga had been presented in *Almayer's Folly*, a younger Lingard would be depicted in *An Outcast*, and a still younger Lingard in the eventual *The Rescue*. In large, medium and small matters, Conrad was fascinated by *hysteron-proteron*, the rhetorical procedure of reversal whereby the later is recounted before the earlier. It is this technique which relates groups of texts (like this Lingard series), covert plotting, oblique narration and delayed decoding. Conrad saw that hysteron-proteron heightened irony and ambiguity, and might imply scepticism about rational order in events. It harmonized, too, with that temperamental inclination to obliquity which had led Conrad to approach the career of a British novelist via years in France and decades of voyages across far oceans. Certainly, hysteron-proteron is evident on a large scale when one notes that his early novels have relatively contemporaneous settings, whereas his last novels (*The Rover* and *Suspense*) deal with the Napoleonic era.

In *An Outcast of the Islands* (1896), Willems, a corrupt egoist who is employed by Lingard, betrays his patron and is drawn to disaster by his infatuation with Aissa. This is another study of the deluded dreamer, of mutual treachery and incommunication, and of Europeans mocked by the exotic terrain. Sexuality, in its possessiveness, is again related to the power-struggles of races and nations; Conrad had told Garnett that the main characters 'are typical of mankind where every individual wishes to assert his power'. In the novel's coda, Almayer, reflecting on the waste of lives, drunkenly voices the narrative's scepticism: 'Where's the sense of all this? Where's your Providence? Where's the good for anybody in all this? The world's a swindle!'

Conrad's confidence in achieving a reputation was confirmed by the reviews of *An Outcast*, which predominantly were highly favourable. Certainly, some reviewers complained of the sordid and depressing nature of the material; several found the book 'wordy', 'over-wrought', slow and prolix; but a recurrent term was 'power'. The *Glasgow Herald*, for instance, concluded:

> *An Outcast of the Islands* is a book of singular and indefinable power; to be read carefully, some times even with labour, but always beautiful in its style, rich alike in passion and in pathos.

Other commentators likened it to fiction by Melville, Victor Hugo, and (as so often) Stevenson and Kipling. 'It is as masculine as Kipling, but without that parade of masculinity which Kipling loves', remarked the *Manchester Guardian*. One of the longest and liveliest of the notices was an anonymous analysis in the *Saturday Review*, which declared:

> *An Outcast of the Islands* is, perhaps, the finest piece of fiction that was published this year, as *Almayer's Folly* was perhaps the finest published in 1895.
>
> Only greatness could make books of which the detailed workmanship was so copiously bad, so well worth reading, so convincing, and so stimulating.

Conrad sent to this reviewer, who was in fact H. G. Wells, a letter of thanks and self-defence, and thus began a sometimes uneasy and guarded friendship between the two men. Later, in *Boon* and *Experiment in Autobiography,* Wells sniped at Conrad's noble literary image and his 'florid mental gestures': 'Conrad "writes". It shows.' Nevertheless, in the 1890s Conrad was a keen admirer of Wells's novels, and *The Time Machine* and *The Island of Doctor Moreau* were to leave their mark on various Conradian texts, notably 'Heart of Darkness' and *The Inheritors.* Wells's complaints about Conrad's prolixity may partly account for the relatively economical manner of *The Nigger of the 'Narcissus',* begun in 1896.

The foundations of Conrad's reputation were now firmly laid, but the financial basis of his literary career was still weak. He had received £20 for *Almayer's Folly;* for *An Outcast,* with its first British edition of 3,000 copies, he received £50 plus around 11 per cent of the proceeds. His inheritance from his uncle, Tadeusz Bobrowski, would not last long, given his gentlemanly life-style and inclination for visits to the continent; and meanwhile his responsibilities had increased. In March 1896 he married Jessie George, a young typist who was to be the mother of Borys Conrad, born in 1898, and John, born in 1906. Jessie, though unsophisticated and uncultured, proved to be a diligent, resourceful and patient wife; but, in her memoirs, written after Conrad's death, she was to vent some long-repressed resentments in anecdotes about her husband's neurotic eccentricities and irascible sensitivity.

The literary career underwent the first of many crises soon after the completion of *An Outcast.* Conrad made a series of false starts. He began a novel entitled *The Sisters,* the story of a sensitive young Slav, an artist who comes to Paris; but only the rather vapid opening was completed. In 1896 he also began *The Rescuer,* the final part of the Lingard trilogy; but its completion was delayed until 1919, when it was serialized (as *The Rescue*) in *Land and Water* magazine. Thomas Moser has persuasively argued that one reason for his difficulties with *The Sisters* and *The Rescuer* was that their subject, romantic love, was largely uncongenial to Conrad's temperament: isolation, incommunication, beleaguered solidarity, political intrigue and maritime crises could elicit his deeper intelligence as grand sexual passion could not. The third false start was 'The Return', which Conrad himself termed 'a left-handed production'. This deals tortuously with the psychological trauma of a wealthy husband on learning of his wife's infidelity. Though prolix, it is a persistently feminist text in its sympathy with the woman who, defying her husband's self-righteous possessiveness, declares: 'I've a right [. . .] to – myself.' (The tale was probably influenced by Ibsen's *A Doll's House*.)

In 1896-7 Conrad published in magazines the very uneven quartet of tales ('Karain', 'The Lagoon', 'The Idiots' and 'An Outpost of Progress') which, with 'The Return', comprise *Tales of Unrest*, issued by Fisher Unwin in 1898. The most impressive of these is certainly 'An Outpost of Progress', which owes a little to Flaubert's *Bouvard et Pécuchet* (1881) and considerably more to Conrad's journey into the Congo Free State. In its mordantly ironic depiction of the self-destructive progress of two European traders (Kayerts and Carlier) in central Africa, it clearly anticipates the satiric boldness of 'Heart of Darkness'. The sardonically relativistic narrator of 'An Outpost' says:

> Few men realize that their life, the very essence of their character, their capabilities and their audacities, are only the expression of their belief in the safety of their surroundings. The courage, the composure, the confidence; the emotions and principles; every great and every insignificant thought belongs not to the individual but to the crowd: to the crowd that believes blindly in the irresistible force of its institutions and of its morals, in the power of its police and of its opinion.

Isolated from such familiar supports, the two traders become demoralized; Kayerts shoots Carlier, and hangs himself from a cross surmounting a grave.

> His toes were only a couple of inches above the ground; his arms hung stiffly down; he seemed to be standing rigidly at attention, but with one purple cheek playfully posed on the shoulder. And, irreverently, he was putting out a swollen tongue at his Managing Director.

The tale, in turn, irreverently puts out its tongue at Belgian imperialism in the Congo, at imperialism generally, and at the hubris of civilization. In the post-Darwinian world of 'An Outpost of Progress', those who are 'fittest to survive' prove to be not the Europeans but the family of Makola from Sierra Leone. Its ironies were heightened by its context: Conrad's story first appeared in the magazine *Cosmopolis* alongside an article by Henry Norman, the political commentator, which declared:

> We are Imperialists first, and Liberals or Tories afterwards. I said this, for my own part, years ago, when the sentiment was not quite so popular. Now it has happily become a commonplace.

3

The Major Phase

FROM *THE NIGGER OF THE 'NARCISSUS'* TO *LORD JIM*

Conrad's major phase as a writer extends from 1897 to 1911, a period of astonishing vigour and versatility in which he produced, among other texts, *The Nigger of the 'Narcissus'*, 'Youth', 'Heart of Darkness', *Lord Jim*, 'Typhoon', *Nostromo, The Secret Agent*, 'The Secret Sharer' and *Under Western Eyes*.

With *The Nigger of the 'Narcissus'* (1897), Conrad seems to have emerged imaginatively from sombre forests into fresh sea air and sunlight. This novel offers a sequence of powerful descriptive set-pieces providing contrast, variety and rapid colourful immediacy. It is much more cinematic (proleptically so, given its date) than his previous novels, the narrator's vision being mobile and widely ranging, now in the forecastle among the quarrelling men of the watch, now on the poop with the officers, and sometimes observing with Olympian detachment the passage of the *Narcissus* across the oceans. Conrad's love of thematic density here becomes intensified in scenes which shimmer between realism, allegory and symbolism. The narrative of the voyage is partly a commemorative tribute to the great days of sail, partly a moral and political allegory of the ways in which a community may be subverted from within by egotism and duplicity, and partly a series of symbolic tableaux epitomizing the price and value of the 'work ethic', the duties and hardships of the sea in contrast to the demeaning pressures of the land, and the right and wrong ways to respond to the threat of death.

If we seek the reasons for this sudden increase in descriptive concision, verve and variety, one may be the nature of the subject-matter: the narrative of a voyage has elicited more of his creative enthusiasm than a narrative of blighted lives on a Bornean coast. Another may be that Conrad had taken note of reviewers' complaints of his prolixity. A third may be his admiration for Stephen Crane's *The Red Badge of Courage* (1895), a brilliantly original impressionistic account of the initiation of young soldiers into the ordeals of warfare. About literary 'impressionism' Conrad was equivocal, sometimes talking as though it were a superficial mode which failed to probe the inner meaning of events, at other times praising Crane with apparently unreserved enthusiasm. On one occasion he termed himself an 'impressionist from instinct', but when he formulated his artistic beliefs in the 'Preface' to *The Nigger,* he made it clear that his ringing declaration, 'My task [. . .] is, before all, to make you *see*', meant that the author should offer insight into the enduring and not merely a vivid rendering of appearances.

Politically, *The Nigger* offers some vigorous Toryism. It is probably Conrad's most right-wing text, and recent critics who see racist implications in the depiction of James Wait, the black seaman from St Kitts, have a strong case. The officers are a sterling team of British seafarers; Donkin, who foments mutiny, is a parasitic pseudo-socialist; James Wait, as his surname implies, is a weight or burden to the white men and the ship; trade-unionism is implicitly scorned; even Samuel Plimsoll's maritime reformers are satirized; and England, though glimpsed as a place of sordid commerce, is hailed oratorically as the 'ship mother of fleets and nations', 'the great flagship of the race'. Conrad had shaped the narrative with W. E. Henley's views in mind. Henley, the friend and patron of Rudyard Kipling, advocated a virile imperialism; and it was in the magazine he edited, *The New Review,* that *The Nigger of the 'Narcissus'* was first published, during the festive year of Queen Victoria's Diamond Jubilee.

When the book appeared, some reviewers were obtuse ('The tale is no tale [. . .] There is no plot', complained the *Daily Mail*), but others praised the novel for its power, vigour and originality. 'Assuredly one of the most powerful and extraordinary books of the year', said the *Star.* In the short term, however, the *Spectator's* reviewer was accurate in his claim that '[Conrad's] choice of themes, and the uncompromising nature of his methods, debar him from attaining a wide popularity'.

Once again, a magazine helped Conrad to survive financially. He formed a friendly relationship with William Blackwood, proprietor of *Blackwood's Edinburgh Magazine* (familiarly known as *Maga*), and with Blackwood's adviser, William Meldrum. Blackwood and

Meldrum took the wise view that though Conrad was not a popular author, he was a genius who would eventually shed retrospective lustre on the venerable periodical which gave him hospitality and generous payment. In the pages of *Maga* appeared 'Karain', 'Youth', 'Heart of Darkness', *Lord Jim*, 'The End of the Tether', and two chapters of *The Mirror of the Sea*.

In 'Youth' (serialized 1898, published in a collection in 1902), Conrad solved a technical problem which had led to inconsistencies in *The Nigger of the 'Narcissus'*: the problem of reconciling the viewpoint of a narrator who has immediate but limited knowledge with that of a narrator who has the reflective scope of hindsight. His solution was to introduce Charles Marlow as the main fictional narrator in a work which uses the 'tale within a tale' device: an anonymous character introduces Marlow, and Marlow then tells a yarn about his earlier days. Such oblique narration was common at that time: among Conrad's acquaintances, it was employed by Henry James, Rudyard Kipling, Cunninghame Graham, Stephen Crane and H. G. Wells. Conrad found the technique particularly congenial. Charles Marlow, who reappears in *Lord Jim*, 'Heart of Darkness' and *Chance*, is the most intelligent, engaging and convincing of Marlow's transtextual characters. (A 'transtextual' character is one who appears in two or more texts, thereby augmenting the realism and range of each.) This weathered sea-captain, fluent as a story-teller, romantic in sympathies yet sceptical in opinions, proved to be a fine enabling device: through Marlow's mask, Conrad could speak freely while reserving options.

'Youth' was a largely autobiographical tale given some romantic, ironic and comic heightening; the factual events were fictionally inflected so as to permit patriotic tributes to British seamanship. It was soon regarded as one of Conrad's finest tales, and its 'purple passages' of descriptive prose were later influentially anthologized; notably the lyrical description of the *Judea's* death by fire at sea. The following extract from the sequence illustrates Conrad's rhetorical romanticism, and particularly that sonorous, poetically alliterative, strongly rhythmic, almost incantatory style (one of many in his range) which, impressing numerous readers in the early twentieth century, came to seem pretentiously 'literary' within a few decades.

> Between the darkness of earth and heaven she was burning fiercely upon a disc of purple sea shot by the blood-red play of gleams; upon a disc of

> water glittering and sinister. A high, clear flame, an immense and lonely flame, ascended from the ocean, and from its summit the black smoke poured continuously at the sky. She burned furiously; mournful and imposing like a funeral pile kindled in the night, surrounded by the sea, watched over by the stars. A magnificent death had come like a grace, like a gift, like a reward to that old ship at the end of her laborious days.

This highly-wrought passage, with its euphonies, inversions, repetitions and parallelisms, can still gratify aural sensualists. Stylistic nostalgia may now compound the elegist's nostalgia for the ship and the bygone era of maritime adventure.

Within eighteen months of 'Youth', *Blackwood's* published 'Heart of Darkness' (February – April 1899), which during the subsequent eighty years became acclaimed as Conrad's supreme work. It is exciting and profound, lucid and bewildering; highly compressed, immensely rich in texture and implication; and it has a recessive adroitness, for its paradoxes repeatedly ambush the conceptualizing reader or critic. Thematically, it holds a remarkably wide range of reference to problems of politics and psychology, morality and religion, social order and evolution. The narrative techniques dextrously imply literary theories which had yet to receive critical formulation: 'defamiliarization' entailing delayed decoding (procedures which challenge conventional understanding), covert plotting (here, the covert rendering of the manager's scheme to eliminate Kurtz), and deconstruction (the exploitation of tension, paradox and contradiction). 'Heart of Darkness' can be related to a diversity of traditions, generic and technical, including political satire, protest literature, traveller's tale, psychological odyssey, symbolic novel, mediated autobiography. Prophetically, it anticipated the follies and brutalities of subsequent history, as was recognized by Francis Ford Coppola's film, *Apocalypse Now* (1979). Written in the heyday of imperialism, it radically challenged the customary justifications of the imperial mission; Victorian in its date, its radicalism of thought and technique made it one of the first great modernist texts. The oblique narrative mode was superbly co-ordinated with several of its themes: one being relativism of perception, another the deceptiveness of language, and yet another the difficulty of adequate comprehension and communication of the significantly unfamiliar.

The compression, sophistication and obliquities of the text are such that it needs to be read several times in order to be properly understood. At a first reading, many ironies are likely to pass unnoticed. We may not see, for example, the significance of the reference to 'the bones' on the first page, or that the 'decent young citizen in a toga' is a portent of Kurtz, or that the wrecking of the steamboat is no accident. Certainly the satiric indictment of colonialism is graphically clear, as is the mockery of the myopic arrogance of the Europeans in daring to impose themselves on the vast alien territory of Africa. Marlow refers to their 'pitiless and rapacious folly', 'with no more moral purpose at the back of it than there is in burglars breaking into a safe'. Many of the 'pilgrims' function as mere avaricious automata; and Kurtz himself (product of 'all Europe', including England), who has brought idealistic ambitions to the wilderness, proves to be depraved and deranged. In its cumulation of images of absurdity, of savage farce, of wanton destruction and demented energy, 'Heart of Darkness' can seem a fiercely pessimistic narrative. Its positive values lie partly in the quality of civilization represented by Marlow, who usually maintains a vigilant humanity; they lie largely in the authorial indignation at man's inhumanity to man, and, indeed, at the despoliation of the earth in the name of 'progress'; and they are richly implicit in the articulate intelligence and virtuosity of the text.

Or so it appeared to many readers in the period 1950–75, when 'Heart of Darkness' received an abundance of tributes from critics who, attuned by modernist literature to complexity, ambiguity and obliquity, rejoiced in its recessive layers of significance and its political and philosophical radicalism. In the later decades of the twentieth century, however, various postcolonial and feminist writers (notably Chinua Achebe and Elaine Showalter) argued that even this text was, after all, tainted by racism and sexism: the Africans and the women were marginalized. There ensued an extensive controversy which demonstrated the importance of relating the text to its original historical and literary context. The merits of any fictional work are, in any case, not necessarily dependent on its endorsement of a reader's prejudices or principles.

Before and after the writing of 'Heart of Darkness', Conrad was working on *Lord Jim*, which was serialized in *Blackwood's* between October 1899 and November 1900. Once again, the glamour and the hubris of a romantic temperament were appraised; once again, imperialism was subjected to critical scrutiny. This novel carries to an extreme Conrad's tendency to take the materials of popular adventure-fiction and give them a distinctively oblique, searching and realistic treatment. By means of time-shifts and mobility of viewpoint, the plot sequence is made deviously and deceptively serpentine, and Jim's character becomes a prism, dividing the various lights shed on him by a diversity of characters. Conrad's own ambivalence in attitude to the romantic egoist is shown by the contrast between the first part of the book, in which Jim's act of cowardice is the centre, and the second part, in which the story of Jim's success on Patusan too greatly resembles an adventure-novel of the kind which had once corrupted the younger Jim. In the closing pages, however, there is a superb recovery of critical balance: Jim dies, having sacrificed himself to the Indonesians who feel betrayed by him, and 'He goes away from a living woman to celebrate his pitiless wedding with a shadowy ideal of conduct'. Jim's death can be seen as both courageous and evasive, both loyal and treacherous, both a vindication of the claims of honour and a submission to 'exalted egoism'. In Jim himself and in the narrative as a whole, romanticism and realism are put into a mutually critical relationship; and the entire work, in all its varied vividness, dramatizes the problem of maintaining constructive ethical conduct in a relativistic world.

When the book of *Lord Jim* was published, most of the reviews were encouraging: the richness and diversity of characterization were frequently praised. A controversial area was the oblique method. The *Sketch*, for example, complained:

> *Lord Jim* is an impossible book – impossible in scheme, impossible in style. It is a short character-sketch, written and re-written to infinity, dissected into shreds, masticated into tastelessness.

The *Speaker*, on the other hand, perceptively observed:

> There is an apparent artlessness about the arrangement of the book which seems to arise from a determination that the reader shall not be led away by the interest of the mere external events of the tale. Events are almost contemptuously forestalled, in order that the how and why of them alone shall get the best attention of the reader. The story doubles back on itself continuously when a theory of conduct wants illustrating and elucidating [. . .] The arrangement of the book is original and effective; it seems to have solved one of the great difficulties of the philosophical romance.

If 'Heart of Darkness' owed some technical and thematic debts to Wells's *The Time Machine* and *The Island of Doctor Moreau*, *Lord Jim* may have been technically indebted to the analytic obliquities of Henry James's fiction as well as to the graphic immediacy of Stephen Crane's; but Conrad, throughout his career, retained a remarkable ability to learn from a diversity of mentors while yet remaining utterly distinctive in his fictional identity. In *Lord Jim*, scene after scene, character after character, endure vividly in the reader's imagination; and, by its intensive ethical analyses and its paradoxical juxtaposition of the public and private, the outer and inner views of a character's crucial action, this novel prepared the way for numerous important literary works (and even some influential films) of the twentieth century.

FROM 'TYPHOON' TO *NOSTROMO*

'Typhoon' was serialized in *Pall Mall Magazine*, 1902, and published in book form as *Typhoon* in New York, 1902, and in *Typhoon and Other Stories* in London, 1903. It was soon recognized as one of Conrad's finest maritime tales. Accounts of a ship's struggle with a storm have long been part of the stock-in-trade of sea-writers; but none of them has surpassed Conrad's description of the *Nan-Shan's* battle with the typhoon. It is graphic, knowledgeable, dramatic. A wealth of vivid particulars brings the vessel's ordeal intensely to the imagination: they range from the darkness that 'palpitated down' between the lightning to the water swallowed by Jukes (now fresh, now salt) while the ship is 'looted by the storm'. Nevertheless, as Conrad said when recalling the incident on which this novella was based,

> the interest [. . .] was, of course, not the bad weather but the extraordinary complication brought into the ship's life at a moment of exceptional stress by the human element below her deck [. . .] I felt that to bring out its deeper significance which was quite apparent to me, something other, something more was required; a leading motive that would harmonize all these violent noises, and a point of view that would put all that elemental fury into its proper place.
>
> What was needed of course was Captain MacWhirr.

The tale stresses that MacWhirr is stolid, unimaginative and unsophisticated; and at first we may be tempted to patronize him as a semi-comic character. Yet the narrative progressively reveals the peculiar integrity which his thick skin both conceals and preserves. He may not have the intelligence or the professionalism to evade the typhoon, but he has the courage to take the ship and her crew through it; he may not understand Jukes's patriotic indignation at serving under a Siamese flag, but when Jukes is almost paralysed by fear, it is MacWhirr who sustains and encourages him. The narrative thus embodies Conrad's 'anti-rational primitivism': the sense that reflection and imagination may incapacitate, whereas simplicity may entail reliability.

Crucially important in 'Typhoon' is MacWhirr's treatment of the 'coolies' (as the Chinese labourers are conventionally termed). Jukes adopts the familiar contemporaneous attitude of racial contempt for them, and, when they panic and brawl during the storm, his inclination is to ignore them. It is MacWhirr who insists that they be restored to salutary order; and again, after the typhoon has passed, it is MacWhirr who is at pains to redistribute their scattered money as equitably as possible. As he explains to Jukes:

> Had to do what's fair, for all – they are only Chinamen. Give them the same chance with ourselves [. . .] Bad enough to be shut up below in a gale [. . .] without being battered to pieces [. . .] Couldn't let that go on in my ship, if I knew she hadn t five minutes to live.

In that gale-interrupted phrase, 'for all – they are only Chinamen', the predictable concession to commonplace racial assumptions is made; but the emphasis falls on MacWhirr's determination to preserve 'fair play' by treating them as fellow humans. The same simple integrity that enables MacWhirr to captain the ship through the typhoon obliges him to enforce a humane order. The 'simple' ethic proves eventually, in its implications and consequences, to be more considerate as well as more practical than Jukes's apparently intelligent outlook. When Jukes rushes about, mustering men with rifles, MacWhirr replies with exasperated common sense: 'For God's sake, Mr. Jukes, [. . .] do take away these rifles from the men. Somebody's sure to get hurt before long if you don't.' At the end of a letter to a friend, Jukes say of MacWhirr: 'I think that he got out of it very well for such a stupid man'; and the irony is that the stupidity here is mainly Jukes's, for failing to see that MacWhirr's reticent simplicity has eventually approximated a model of humane practicality.

MacWhirr's wife impatiently skims the letters she receives, unable to imagine the ship's perils or to appreciate her husband's courage. The tale suggests what she may never learn: the ordeals faced, in the course of wage-earning, by those whose labours are taken for granted; and the salutary integrity of obscure and unglamorous individuals whose heroism is not the less for its absence of egoistic eloquence.

Some readers of 'Typhoon' may now deem Conrad's presentation of the Chinese culturally patronizing, given that only a European can master their internecine panic; others may deem it plausibly consistent, given the thematic need to dramatize their confusion as a daunting challenge. Similarly, some may find the tale's political implications authoritarian, suggesting that a strong leader is needed to meet the threat of social anarchy, while others may find them democratic, given that the thick-skinned mariner from a humble background proves equal to a variety of responsibilities and becomes the mentor of his socially advantaged first mate. Whatever the verdict, the linguistic richness of 'Typhoon' mocks the grey prose of a summary.

If 'Heart of Darkness' is the greatest of Conrad's *novelle* or longer tales, *Nostromo* is the greatest of his novels. Audaciously immense and complex in scale and scope, this psycho-political work (interconnecting personal desires and global politics) depicts graphically the crucial phase in the evolution of a South American republic: the phase in which, as a consequence of European and North American capital investment and enterprise, Sulaco ceases to be a province of a strife-torn region and becomes a new state with its democratic institutions and civilized amenities. Near the end of the saga, Captain Mitchell is able to look with complacent pride on the new republic, with its railways, department-stores and clubs. To him, an era of poverty and futile civil wars seems finally to have been superseded by a tranquil era in which, under parliamentary government, property-owners like himself can look forward to a peaceful retirement enhanced by the income from their shares in the San Tomé silver-mine, while, in his view, the masses can enjoy peace, security, and a steadily improving material standard of living. It is typical of Conrad's janiform outlook that, while parts of the text support Mitchell's optimism, other parts offer ominous forebodings. Dr Monygham, for example, says:

> There is no peace and no rest in the development of material interests.

> They have their law, and their justice. But it is founded on expediency, and is inhuman; it is without rectitude, without the continuity and the force that can be found only in a moral principle. Mrs. Gould, the time approaches when all that the Gould Concession stands for shall weigh as heavily upon the people as the barbarism, cruelty and misrule of a few years back.

And Mrs Gould accepts his wisdom:

> She saw the San Tomé mountain hanging over the Campo, over the whole land, feared, hated, wealthy; more soulless than any tyrant, more pitiless and autocratic than the worst Government; ready to crush innumerable lives in the expansion of its greatness.

Like 'Heart of Darkness', though on a more panoramic scale, *Nostromo* displays Conrad's prophetically acute political intelligence. Here he adroitly depicts the inevitability, the merits and the perils of economic imperialism. With incisive verve, he shows how economics can be regarded as a key to history, the quest for material gain providing the main structure beneath the cultural superstructure; he suggests that in the long term the success of men's schemes depends upon their compatibility with international economic forces; and he illustrates the ways in which a state's political apparatus can be manipulated in the interests of the wealthy. In the essay 'Autocracy and War' (1905), Conrad declares:

> Industrialism and commercialism [. . .] stand ready, almost eager, to appeal to the sword as soon as the globe of the earth has shrunk beneath our growing numbers by another ell or so. And democracy, which has elected to pin its faith to the supremacy of material interests, will have to fight their battles to the bitter end, on a mere pittance [. . .]
>
> The intellectual stage of mankind being as yet in its infancy, and States, like most individuals, having but a feeble and imperfect consciousness of the worth and force of the inner life, the need of making their existence manifest to themselves is determined in the direction of physical activity. The idea of ceasing to grow in territory, in strength, in wealth, in influence – in anything but wisdom and self-knowledge [–] is odious to them as the omen of an end. Action, in which is to be found the illusion of a mastered destiny, can alone satisfy our uneasy vanity and lay to rest the haunting fear of the future [. . .] It will be long before we have learned that in the great darkness before us there is nothing that we need fear.

This Olympian view of striving yet immature humans, impelled to impose themselves on the mockingly vast environment while ultimately doomed to extinction, is the source of the major ironies of *Nostromo*. Repeatedly, individuals are ambushed by their own endeavours, defeated by their own apparent successes: Charles Gould, unable to recognize that the mine, which he owns, effectively owns him and corrupts his judgement; Gian' Battista Nostromo, imprisoned by his vanity, enslaved by the silver which he so successfully steals; Martin Decoud, driven to suicide by the scepticism which reduces all things to 'a succession of incomprehensible images'. Repeatedly the events illustrate the narrator's witheringly cynical maxim:

> In our activity alone do we find the sustaining illusion of an independent existence as against the whole scheme of things of which we form a helpless part.

As an American critic (Albert Guerard) later remarked, Conrad's view of history 'is skeptical and disillusioned, which for us today must mean true'.

Yet although, in paraphrase, *Nostromo* offers a dauntingly pessimistic view of human political endeavours, the novel as a whole is exuberantly and richly vital. With an astonishingly resourceful grasp of the particular and the general, Conrad brings his fictional Sulaco to vivid life: again and again, powerfully visualized scenes, locations and individuals bombard the imagination: the social panorama is dense, turbulent, diverse, striking. The orchestrated effects include the sombre, the farcical, the poignant, the drily ironic, the absurd and the tragic. Conrad's range of voices extends from the grotesque rhetoric of Pedrito Montero to the incisive wit of Decoud and the resonant eloquence of the narrator. Given that Conrad's native language was Polish, the linguistic virtuosity of the text is audacious; given that he had only briefly visited South America, the creation of so convincing a fictional landscape is a triumph of assimilated research and the co-ordinating imagination. Only towards the close of the novel, in the depiction of Nostromo's fatal attraction to Giselle Viola, do the prose and plotting decline towards the melodramatic.

In its technical innovations, *Nostromo* was highly ambitious. It combined extreme temporal mobility with mobility of viewpoint. The time-shifts boldly juxtapose and interweave the past, present and future; and the shifts in viewpoint also multiply perspectives, offering now a diminishing view from the skies, now a magnifying close-up, so that humans are dwarfed or loom large. Ironies are multiplied by the diversity of informants: even the Olympian narrator proves to be not fully reliable. Once again, a significant number of the early reviewers were baffled by these technical challenges. 'The plot is confused', said the *British Weekly*; 'the tale does not run smoothly from incident to incident; it is often difficult to say when or where we are'; and the *Manchester Guardian* encountered 'what seems an arbitrary and baffling design'. Gradually, during the subsequent sixty years, critics (educated by the achievements of modernist writers) came to perceive the logic of the method. Conrad's technical devices heighten irony, give prominence to thematic co-ordination, and offer a sceptical searching of experience. In the 'Author's Note', Conrad says that the book displays 'the passions of men short-sighted in good and evil'. By delaying the decoding of events, Conrad obliges the reader to share the myopia of the characters; and by provoking the decoding, he provides the therapy which helps us to share his own keen vision. We distort the novel's meaning if we over-emphasize either the initial chronological flux or the resolved chronological order.

Nostromo both shows and evokes what a semiotician, Michael Riffaterre, has called 'the praxis of the transformation': the very activity of making significant order. A strong patterning of events emerges, but only after we have experienced the recalcitrance of events; a clear historical viewpoint is established, but only after we have been shown the ways in which recorded history may falsify actions by smoothing the knobbly awkwardness of their impact; and a sombre view of human capacities emerges, but only after we have seen vivid instances of the particular needs, drives and sufferings of a variety of humans. The novel dramatizes the ironic disparity between the two senses of 'history', which can mean both 'events which actually occurred' and 'a historian's selective account of events which are supposed to have occurred'. Thus, *Nostromo* is a fictional history whose methods cast doubt on the human veracity – the fidelity to the texture of life – of orthodox historians. Conrad said that in a novel, the 'accumulated verisimilitude of selected episodes puts to shame the pride of documentary history': so he would have agreed fully with the spirit of Aristotle's remark, 'Poetry, therefore, is more philosophical and of higher value than history'.

In the essay 'Art as Technique' (1917), Viktor Shklovsky claimed that habitual perception destroys; as we take things for granted, they die to us; but the artist uses a variety of 'defamiliarization devices' to surprise us into a fresh apprehension of reality. Shklovsky did not refer to Conrad, but in his major phase Conrad was a master of a wide range of techniques which defamiliarize human experience. When the techniques of *Nostromo* have opened our eyes, we may finally look upon that novel not as 'a succession of incomprehensible images', but rather as the engineer looked upon Mount Higuerota, 'thinking that in this sight, as in a piece of inspired music, there could be found together the utmost delicacy of shaded expression and a stupendous magnificence of effect'.

FROM *THE SECRET AGENT* TO *UNDER WESTERN EYES*

The Secret Agent (serial, 1906–7; book 1907) is the most tautly plotted and elegantly stylized of Conrad's political novels. Highly ironic, strongly satiric, sombre yet tinged with black comedy or savage farce, this study of anarchists and conspirators in Victorian London is an important intermediary text: intermediary between the urban fictions of Charles Dickens and those of Graham Greene, between vivid grotesquerie and seedy corruption. A remarkable characterization is the impersonal narrator: urbane, drily ironic or sardonic, inspecting human vice and folly with the amused contempt of a disenchanted connoisseur. Here, for example, he dissects the character of Adolf Verloc, the double agent and betrayer of revolutionaries:

> Protection is the first necessity of opulence and luxury [. . .]; the whole social order favourable to their hygienic idleness had to be protected against the shallow idleness of unhygienic labour. It had to – and Mr. Verloc would have rubbed his hands with satisfaction had he not been constitutionally averse from every superfluous exertion. His idleness was not hygienic, but it suited him very well. He was in a manner devoted to it with a sort of inert fanaticism, or perhaps rather with a fanatical inertness. Born of industrious parents for a life of toil, he had embraced indolence from an impulse as profound as inexplicable and as imperious as the impulse which directs a man's preference for one particular woman in a given thousand.

Verloc, Ossipon, Yundt, Michaelis, the Professor: all these conspirators are seen as lazy, grotesque and parasitic, their endeavours futile and self-defeating. Although the British empire, we are reminded, is 'the Empire on which the sun never sets', at the centre of

London is Verloc's sordid shop 'where the sun never shone'; and London is depicted predominantly as dark, dank, slimy and oppressive. Where there is altruism, it results only in disaster. Thus, Winnie has married Adolf Verloc in order to secure a protector for her retarded half-brother, Stevie, and her mother has retired to an old persons' home to ensure that Verloc can maintain that protection; but the consequence is Stevie's death when carrying a bomb for his brother-in-law. Eventually, after killing Verloc, Winnie drowns herself in the English Channel. Though the forces of law and order eventually prevail, they do so with tarnished integrity: for example, the Assistant Commissioner succeeds in unmasking the villain, Vladimir, partly as a result of endeavouring to safeguard the interests of a wealthy lady who has befriended his wife.

Superbly crafted, technically assured, *The Secret Agent* remains bleak in its cumulative emphasis on destruction and futility. In 1948, however, F. R. Leavis claimed that this novel was 'one of Conrad's two supreme masterpieces, one of the two unquestionable classics of the first order that he added to the English novel' (the other being *Nostromo*). Leavis's enthusiasm had been largely anticipated by some of the earliest reviewers. The review in the *Glasgow News* was headed 'A Great Book', and postulated its 'profound and comprehensive knowledge of human nature'; Edward Garnett found further evidence of 'Conrad's superiority over nearly all contemporary English novelists'; and the *Star* declared:

> Since Dickens no novelist has caught the obscure haunting grotesquerie of London. Now Mr. Conrad has caught it, and caught it as wonderfully as he caught the magic of the Malay forest and the magic of the sea.

Other reviewers, however, found *The Secret Agent* ugly and sordid: *Country Life* had 'no hesitation in saying that the whole thing is indecent'; and these adverse comments remained the dominant ones in Conrad's memory, to judge from his remarks in 1920:

> Some of the admonitions were severe, others had a sorrowful note [. . .] It seems to me now that even an artless person might have foreseen that some criticisms would be based on the ground of sordid surroundings and the moral squalor of the tale [. . .]
>
> But still I will submit that [. . .] I have not intended to commit a gratuitous outrage on the feelings of mankind.

Meanwhile, Conrad continued his production of maritime tales.

He disliked being termed 'a writer of the sea'; and the distinction between his maritime works and his political works is rather specious, since he was often most seductively political when depicting the relationship between captain and crew. This is well illustrated by 'The Secret Sharer', originally published in *Harper's Monthly Magazine* in 1910 and later included in *'Twixt Land and Sea* (1912). Generally regarded as one of Conrad's finest tales, it has attracted numerous and diverse interpretations. It is lucid, concise, tense, exciting and strange; and morally it holds a grittily resistant feature. The merit of a literary text may lie in its qualities of articulate intelligence, and its paraphrasable morality may be harsher than a critic might wish it to be.

'The Secret Sharer' is a tale which succeeds in being at once satisfyingly straightforward and intriguingly mysterious. After the deceptive calm of the opening, there follows the shock provided by the unexpected visitant, the suspense aroused by the young captain's endeavour to conceal the fugitive, and the climactic suspense entailed by the captain's determination to take his ship perilously close to a rocky shore while the fugitive escapes. The narrative is terse and economical, and our interest is engaged by a relay-race of questions. Who is the fugitive? How can he be successfully concealed? Will the captain succeed in mastering the new ship while yet helping the law-breaker? And will the vessel finally survive the manoeuvre? Broadly, the central principle of suspense is that the evidence to support a reader's prediction of a *successful* outcome is almost evenly matched by evidence to support a prediction of a *disastrous* outcome. The story is well paced; every detail counts; numerous ironies are generated; and the sense of conspiratorial confinement (and, finally, of wilfully perilous navigation) is admirably evoked.

What makes the tale so tempting to read and reread, and what makes it so seductive to commentators, is the fact that while, as narrative sequence, it is lucidly straightforward, it generates a variety of enigmas, connotations and problems. Obviously, it has the resonance of a work which extends the *Doppelgänger* tradition. This literary tradition burgeoned in the Romantic period and continued through the nineteenth century into the twentieth. Representative texts include Poe's 'William Wilson', Dostoevsky's 'The Double' and Stevenson's 'Dr Jekyll and Mr Hyde'. The main convention in such texts is that an uncanny complicity is established between two apparently contrasting characters: their relationship is symbiotic. The captain says that Leggatt, the fugitive, 'was not a bit like me, really', yet Leggatt also seems 'part of myself', 'my other self', 'my secret self' and 'my double'. Conrad's enduring interest in kinship between a protagonist and an outlaw gains here its most explicit presentation. (We may recall related aspects of *The Nigger*, 'Heart of Darkness', *Lord Jim* and, later, *Under Western Eyes* and *Victory*.) Some of the reasons for the bond between the hero and Leggatt are obvious enough: both are young British 'gentlemen-officers' who have served on the training-ship *Conway*; socially superior to their fellow seamen, they are bound by caste and class. The bond is also a matter of immediate, intuitive understanding, slightly tinged with the homo-erotic. As is 'love at first sight' in the realm of emotions (instant, strong, irrational), so is their empathy in the realm of ethics. The stress on strange kinship has encouraged various critics to see Leggatt as some kind of Freudian 'id' or Jungian 'anima', as a repressed part of the hero's psyche, but this endeavour is resisted by the narrative's predominant realism, which establishes fully the external existence of Leggatt. The tale does, however, adumbrate lightly (as a flickering glow of suggestion) a supernatural covert plot, in which Leggatt seems a ghostly visitant to be encountered and exorcized. Koh-ring, the island to which Leggatt finally swims, is described as an Erebus, a gateway to the underworld. When Leggatt remarks, 'It would never do for me to come to life again', the narrator comments: 'It was something that a ghost might had said.'

We are told that Leggatt swims away 'to take his punishment'. At the realistic level, this remark is true only in the sense that he has chosen to begin a self-imposed exile as a fugitive. In the most obvious sense, however, the remark is a lie, since Leggatt is fleeing the punishment that would assuredly await him if he were put on trial for homicide. Indeed, one of the most enigmatic features of the tale is that the narrator never seems to appreciate the moral enormity of his own readiness to help a felon to elude justice. Leggatt killed a man who impeded his endeavour to set a sail during a storm. He believes himself to be entirely justified in his homicidal action, since the sail saved the imperilled ship. The hero unquestioningly accepts Leggatt's view. An unsavoury moral implication is clearly that some men constitute a bold élite with the right to override long-established moral and legal principles. One elegant structural and ethical irony of the tale is that whereas Leggatt had thought it right to kill a man in order to save a ship and her crew, the hero thinks it right to imperil a ship and her crew in order to save a man. As Leggatt resembles a complementary mirror-image of the hero, so the eventual crisis on the young captain's vessel resembles a complementary mirror-image of the crisis on Leggatt's vessel.

The structural elegance of 'The Secret Sharer' is also illustrated by the detail of the 'white hat' in the sea. When Leggatt is about to escape overboard, the captain impulsively pushes his own floppy white hat on to the fugitive's head (so that it might later shield him from the tropical sun ashore); but the hat, falling off as Leggatt plunges into the waves, forms the salutary marker which, by showing that the ship is gathering sternway, helps the captain to avert shipwreck in the darkness. The kindly gift has rewarded the giver, just as the captain's risky protection of Leggatt has culminated in a test of seamanship which enables the captain to gain confidence in his own authority over the ship. Like *The Shadow-Line,* this is both the story of initiation by ordeal into maturity and a mystification of maritime command. Lucid and elegant, 'The Secret Sharer' is both a vivid yarn and a tantalizing rune. By depicting complicity with a violent outlaw as a near-mystical imperative with a valuably positive outcome, it displays in extreme form the defiantly romantic and almost Nietzschian aspect of Conrad's paradoxical temperament; and it neatly complements the treatment of the fugitive in *Under Western Eyes.*

Conrad once remarked: 'Fraternity means nothing unless the Cain-Abel business'; in 'The Secret Sharer', the hero fraternally befriends a modern Cain. Perhaps E. M. Forster recalled the story when he declared: 'If I had to choose between betraying my country and betraying my friend, I hope I should have the guts to betray my country.' 'The Secret Sharer' remains a feat of imagination, not a manifesto; a creative hypothesis, not a testament.

Between December 1907 and January 1910 Conrad had completed the manuscript of *Under Western Eyes,* which, like *Lord Jim, Nostromo* and *The Secret Agent,* had originally been envisaged as a short story. Completion of the new novel was marked by an acute psychological breakdown: his wife, Jessie, reported with ungrammatical immediacy:

> Poor Conrad is very ill and Dr Hackney says it will be a long time before he is fit for anything requiring mental exertion [. . .] There is the M.S.

> complete but uncorrected and his fierce refusal to let even I touch it. It lays on a table at the foot of the bed and he lives mixed up in the scenes and holds converse with the characters [. . .]

Several factors contributed to this breakdown. One was a quarrel with J. B. Pinker, his long-suffering literary agent, who had been providing cheques of £6 per week and had become exasperated by the slow progress of *Under Western Eyes*. (The author's debts now totalled £2,250, at a time when the average income of a doctor or dentist would approximate £380 per annum.) Conrad had also quarrelled with his erstwhile collaborator, Ford Madox Hueffer. But the main factor was, almost certainly, the imaginative and emotional strain entailed by the writing of a novel which related so directly to the sufferings of Conrad's childhood.

Under Western Eyes attempts to treat in a cool, impartial manner both the evils of the autocratic régime in tsarist Russia and the follies and myopia of the revolutionaries opposed to that régime. Although some of the characters (notably Mme de S-, Peter Ivanovitch and the double agent Nikita) are depicted with a satiric vigour reminiscent of *The Secret Agent*, the novel as a whole is written in a more realistic, scrupulous and meditative mode. Just as there are careful gradations in the representatives of tsarism (Prince K- being far more sympathetic than Councillor Mikulin), so, among the revolutionary group, Natalia Haldin and Sophia Antonovna are shown as genuine idealists in contrast to the charlatan, Peter Ivanovitch. One pessimistic political thesis of the book recalls the essay 'Autocracy and War': though the repressive autocracy inevitably generates revolutionary conspiracies, a revolution is likely to result only in a new dictatorship. The narrator echoes Conrad's beliefs when he says:

> A violent revolution falls into the hands of narrow-minded fanatics and of tyrannical hypocrites at first. Afterwards comes the turn of all the pretentious intellectual failures of the time. Such are the chiefs and the leaders. You will notice that I have left out the mere rogues. The scrupulous and the just, the noble, humane, and devoted natures; the unselfish and the intelligent may begin a movement – but it passes away from them. They are not the leaders of a revolution. They are its victims: the victims of disgust, of disenchantment – often of remorse. Hopes grotesquely betrayed, ideals caricatured – that is the definition of revolutionary success.

In formulating such views, Conrad would have in mind the decline of the French Revolution from the era of 'Liberty, Equality, Fraternity' to the time of the Terror and the eventual emergence of Napoleon as dictator-emperor: this would form part of the subject-matter of *The Rover* and *Suspense*. In 1920, three years after the Russian 'October Revolution', Conrad added to *Under Western Eyes* an 'Author's Note' which declared that he had been vindicated by history:

> The ferocity and imbecility of an autocratic rule rejecting all legality and, in fact, basing itself upon complete moral anarchism provokes the no less imbecile and atrocious answer of a purely Utopian revolutionism encompassing destruction by the first means to hand, in the strange conviction that a fundamental change of hearts must follow the downfall of any given human institution [. . .] The oppressors and the oppressed are all Russians together, and the world is brought once more face to face with the truth of the saying that the tiger cannot change his stripes nor the leopard his spots.

Notwithstanding the differences between Poles fighting the Russians for national independence and Russian conspirators seeking the overthrow of tsarism, the novel's thesis about the corruptibility of revolutionary ideals would inevitably have entailed painful reflections for Conrad about the patriotic idealism of his parents; and the plight of the central character had some connections with Conrad's early situation. Razumov, isolated, lonely, seeking to win a silver medal for an essay and thereby to pursue an academic career, finds himself forced to choose between two undesirable political alternatives: either complicity in assassination, or betrayal of a conspirator to the authorities. Having betrayed the assassin, Victor Haldin, he steps not into freedom but into servitude, obliged to serve the autocratic régime as a spy. Conrad had been able to emigrate from tsarism and, by changing his nationality, to cancel the legal obligation to serve the Russian state; for Razumov there is only the way of duplicity, confession, punishment and reclusive retreat. Razumov's watchwords had been: 'History not Theory. Patriotism not Internationalism. Evolution not Revolution. Direction not Destruction. Unity not Disruption.' Conrad's Polish biographer, Zdzisław Najder, comments:

> Conrad had every sympathy with the first group of watchwords, but at the same time he saw clearly that within the realm of tsarist Russia these

principles were thoroughly pernicious. Thus he had to struggle – to no avail – with his own deeply rooted opinions.

The early, Russian scenes of the novel (snowy St Petersburg, with its extremes of squalor and opulence) are among Conrad's finest, and Jocelyn Baines has remarked that 'the characters [. . .] are more subtly and convincingly developed than those in any other of Conrad's novels'. Inevitably, *Under Western Eyes* invites comparison with *Crime and Punishment*. Though Conrad regarded Dostoevsky as 'the grimacing, haunted creature' evoking 'fierce mouthings from prehistoric ages', there are clear links between the two works. Most obviously, in each case the central character (initially a student at St Petersburg) is tortured by memory of his crime and eventually confesses his guilt. Raskolnikov is impelled towards confession by the idealistic and loving Sonya, whose appearance reminds him of Lizaveta, whom he had killed. Razumov is similarly impelled by the idealistic and loving Natalia, whose appearance reminds him of Victor, for whose death he was responsible. Both protagonists are lonely, introspective, intelligent, neurotic, bad-tempered and sardonically contemptuous of others. Both undergo repeated interviews with an astute representative of the police; in each case the interviewer sees more deeply into the truth of the matter than the exasperated interviewee expects. In addition to similarities in the plots, there are numerous verbal echoes: even the name Razumov, which means 'Son of Reason', seems to have been suggested by the name of Raskolnikov's friend Razumikhin – a surname which, another character remarks, 'deriving as it does from the word "reason" [. . .] leads me to believe that he must be a student of theology'.

Nevertheless, the relationship between Conrad's novel and Dostoevsky's is more often critical than derivative. Conrad offers a relatively concise narrative. The confessional garrulity of many of Dostoevsky's characters is implicitly criticized not only by the more economical dialogue of Conrad's but also by the language teacher's strictures on the Russians' 'extraordinary love of words'. In contrast to Dostoevsky's concluding Christian emphasis on confession as a key to redemption and joyful regeneration, Conrad concludes with a sombre and relatively secular emphasis on disillusionment and withdrawal from struggle: Razumov becomes a reclusive invalid, Natalia turns from revolutionary conspiracy to charitable visiting, and the arch-conspirator Peter Ivanovitch opts for quiet married life with 'a peasant girl'. Above all, Conrad vindicates the title *Under Western Eyes* by lucidly depicting what Dostoevsky (who revered tsarism) could not: the relationship between violent revolt and the oppressive autocratic system. Instead of the turbulently volatile emotional bounty with which Dostoevsky renders the interaction of lives which are so often tormented, desperate and anguished, Conrad strives for a more austere, lucid and ironic overview of lives distorted and riven by political ideologies. Yet there remains common ground: Razumov, in temperament, in his bitter alienation and in his eventual confessional accession to the claims of truthful humanity, resembles a twin brother of the lonely Raskolnikov.

When the book appeared in October 1911, it received some very laudatory reviews, and sales in both Britain and the USA were somewhat better than those of *The Secret Agent*. In London, 3,000 copies of *Under Western Eyes* were issued; in New York, 4,000; and British sales in the two years after publication totalled 4,112 copies. Najder has estimated that Conrad's income was now about £600 per annum, including a Civil List pension of £100 each year (awarded in August 1910 'in consideration of his merits as a writer of fiction'). Nevertheless, his debts increased; as ever, Conrad seemed compelled to live beyond his means.

COLLABORATION WITH HUEFFER

During his major phase, there was a clear bifurcation in Conrad's output. Part of his time was devoted to work of integrity: taxing, original texts which might appeal to discerning readers and, eventually, to posterity. But another part of his time was allotted to the rapid production of material for sale: slight tales, potboilers, and, above all, the collaboration-jobs with Ford Madox Hueffer: 'our partnership – in crime', as Conrad called it.

Conrad brought to their collaboration his acumen, his high literary prestige and a variety of useful contacts in the world of publishing. What Hueffer brought was his youthful energy, a mind full of fancies and speculative schemes, and an easy fluency as a writer. In the event, neither substantial commercial success nor critical prestige rewarded their partnership. *The Inheritors*, a mixture of science fiction and topical political allegory, appeared in 1901, and *Romance*, a novel of piracy and passion, in 1903; in both cases, much of the writing was Hueffer's. A tale, 'The Nature of a Crime', was originally published in the *English Review* (which Hueffer edited) under the pseudonym 'Baron Ignatz von Aschendrof'. Although the autobiographical *The Mirror of the Sea* was advertised as Conrad's alone, six of its fifteen divisions were largely the work of Hueffer, who acted as prompter, amanuensis and elaborator. A small part of the manuscript of *Nostromo* is in his handwriting; and Hueffer may have furnished some parts of 'The End of the Tether'. He provided the bases of the tales 'Amy Foster' and 'To-morrow', and helped Conrad convert the latter into a one-act play. Incidentally, though often short of funds himself, Hueffer joined the long roll of honour of Conradian creditors.

As founder-editor of the *English Review*, he helped to establish literary modernism by giving space to Ezra Pound, T. S. Eliot and D. H. Lawrence. His own best work is the novel *The Good Soldier* (1915). After serving on the battlefields of the Great War, he changed his name in 1919 to Ford Madox Ford. Subsequently, while founder-editor of *Transatlantic Review*, he published work by Gertrude Stein, Ernest Hemingway, E. E. Cummings and James Joyce. His recollections of Conrad, in *Joseph Conrad: A Personal Remembrance* and *Return to Yesterday*, were to prove unreliable but lively, as he avowedly aimed for accuracy of impression rather than of fact. Though the two men had eventually quarrelled, Ford had helped to sustain Conrad during excruciatingly difficult years; and the vanity of the reminiscences is outweighed by their affectionate admiration for the senior author.

4

Transition: 1911–19

The period 1911–19 was in two senses, for Conrad, a period of transition. First, while some of the novels and tales of this period are impressive, others show a marked decline in Conrad's powers; and, secondly, there was to be a spectacular improvement in his income.

In order, the main publications of this phase are: *A Personal Record* (originally *Some Reminiscences*), issued as a book in 1912 after prior serialization, and by far the more interesting of his two books of autobiographical reflections; *'Twixt Land and Sea*, 1912 (three tales, including 'The Secret Sharer'); *Chance*, serialized in the *New York Herald* in 1912 and published as a book early in 1914; *Victory*, serials and book, 1915; *Within the Tides* (four of his more trivial tales), 1915; and *The Shadow-Line*, serialized 1916–17, the book appearing in 1917.

The short stories in the collections are remarkably uneven in quality, ranging from the admirable 'The Secret Sharer' and 'A Smile of Fortune' to the lamentable 'Freya of the Seven Isles' and 'The Inn of the Two Witches', an old-fashioned melodramatic yarn reminiscent of Wilkie Collins's 'A Terribly Strange Bed'. Of the novels in this period, most critics concur in regarding *The Shadow-Line* as the best: a powerful study of the stresses on a young captain whose first command is a disease-haunted and becalmed sailing-ship. In the 'Author's Note', Conrad denied that the novel held any supernatural elements; nevertheless, like 'The Secret Sharer', *The Shadow-Line* depends for its force largely on an evocation of supernatural possibilities. The narrative, which holds strong allusions to Coleridge's 'Rime of the Ancyent Marinere' and to the legend of the Flying Dutchman, is at one level a story of curse and exorcism, while at the secular level it tells of the need to defend self-discipline from the subversive forces of guilt and supersition.

The novel which most deeply affected Conrad's fortunes was *Chance*. Until then, Conrad's debt to J. B. Pinker remained great, and the author had also needed help from the British taxpayer in the form of grants from the Royal Literary Fund and a Civil List pension. *Chance*'s success in the market may initially seem hard to explain. This is not one of Conrad's best novels; nor is it obviously 'popular' in method, for the narrative is unfolded with serpentine deviousness, and this obliqueness often appears gratuitous rather than illuminating. The *New York Herald,* however, had given prominent and astute publicity to its serialization of the novel in 1912. Repeatedly the magazine stressed that the great novelist had written this work especially for the *New York Herald* and its *female* readers. Women had long constituted a majority of the fiction-reading public (as they still do today); previously, Conrad's fiction had seemed particularly masculine in its orientation. The publicity-campaign modified Conrad's public image. When the book appeared, its jacket featured an attractive young woman with an attentive naval officer at her side, implying that *Chance* would be a love-story. Like the serial, the book was zealously publicized in the United States: a Conrad enthusiast in a key position was Alfred Knopf, who persuaded his employer (F. N. Doubleday) to promote the novel lavishly; and Knopf elicited quotable tributes to the author from many cultural celebrities. Conrad was shrewd when he told Pinker: 'It's the sort of stuff that *may* have a chance with the public. All of it about a girl and with a steady run of references to women in general all along [. . .] It ought to go down.' Given the feminist upsurge in the period 1905–14, there was obvious topicality in the running discussion of 'woman's nature' and in the satiric depiction both of the lesbian Mrs Fyne and of Carleon Anthony, a domestic tyrant whose poetry idealizes women. (He was based partly on Coventry Patmore, author of *The Angel in the House*.) The novel's central interest was the embattled psychology of a young woman making her lonely and arduous journey to fulfilment in marriage. Furthermore, the main love-story's dénouement was, by Conradian standards, unusually happy, with the inhibited hero and heroine eventually experiencing their long-delayed sexual embrace.

When that heroine, Flora de Barral, and her father are described by the narrator as 'Figures from Dickens – pregnant with pathos', the reference is apt, given that the plot of *Chance* holds echoes of *Dombey and Son* and *Little Dorrit*. In its narrative obliquity and teasing ambiguities, it is also indebted to Henry James; and there are clear links between *Chance* and 'The Turn of the Screw', for both works feature a victimized child called Flora and a governess with an unsavoury lover. When reviewing *Chance*, Henry James complained (in laboriously elaborate sentences) that its techniques were elaborately laborious. He was not alone in this complaint; but other reviewers were more generous, and *Chance* received widespread and prominent coverage.

In the month of its appearance, January 1914, *Lord Jim* was reissued, this time in a large popular edition: 15,000 copies priced at one shilling. In the wake of *Chance*'s success, publishers hastened to reprint more of the earlier works; soon, collected editions (by Doubleday in the United States and by Heinemann and Dent in Britain) would appear; manuscript collectors wooed Conrad; and Hollywood provided a new market for authors – particularly authors who, like Conrad, had provided adventurous narratives set in exotic locations.

Victory is a novel which, in its setting and situations (tropical island, 'fallen woman' living with gallant rescuer, invasion by three desperadoes, attempted rape, spectacular conflagration), gives the impression of being aimed at Hollywood; and, if that was Conrad's aim, he hit the target three times, for *Victory* was filmed in 1919, 1930 and 1940. This novel resumes many of the themes that had characterized the earlier fiction: isolation and incommunication; reflection as the foe of practical activity; benevolent patronage which proves destructive; complicity between the well-meaning person and the outlaw. Thus, there are echoes of Decoud in *Nostromo*, of Lingard in *An Outcast*, of Lord Jim and his encounter with Gentleman Brown. Yet *Victory* demonstrates that, in a work of literature, the value of a theme depends on its quality of embodiment. The novel begins promisingly with the depiction of the reclusive Heyst and the web of misunderstanding woven about him, but the tone falters towards conventionality in the sexual relationship between Heyst and Lena, and, with the arrival of the grotesque trio of villains (Jones, Ricardo and Pedro), Conrad offers melodrama compounded with pretentiously allegorical rhetoric. To many current readers, Jones seems too spectrally satanic, Ricardo too feline and Pedro too simian for belief. (Since the appearance of Cornelius and Gentleman Brown in *Lord Jim*, a recurrent weakness in Conradian fiction had been the caricatural depiction of villainy.) The death of Lena, who sacrifices her life to prove her love for the man who had rescued her, is derivative not only from Stefan Żeromski's *The History of a Sin* but also from a long line of romantic novels and operas. This radically flawed work nevertheless consolidated Conrad's popularity.

Even when in debt, Conrad had never stinted himself: he had dressed like a dandy or rural squire, owned a succession of expensive early motor cars, and rented increasingly large houses; but now, at last, his income was more than adequate for his life-style. His agent had been able to obtain advances for *Victory* of £1,000 for the serial rights (*Munsey's Magazine*) and £850 for the book. The money helped Conrad to take his family on a visit to Poland in 1914; but the sentimental journey to Kraków and Zakopane was disrupted by the outbreak of the Great War, and it was with extreme difficulty that the family eluded internment, returning to England via Italy. Ironically, it was a war that Conrad had long prophesied; and his own son Borys served as an officer at the front, was gassed and shell-shocked. After the Armistice, Conrad was pessimistic about the prospects of the newly founded League of Nations, but at least could take consolation from the re-establishment of the Polish State – a reborn republic.

5

Decline

In the closing years of his life, Conrad's main publications were *The Arrow of Gold* (serialized 1918–20, published as a book in 1919), *The Rescue* (serials, 1919–20, book, 1920), *Notes on Life and Letters* (1921, a collection of essays and occasional pieces) and *The Rover* (serial and book, 1923). Posthumously published volumes were *Suspense* (never completed), *Tales of Hearsay* and *Last Essays*. All four novels of this last phase have disappointing aspects: in *The Arrow of Gold* and particularly in *The Rescue* and *Suspense*, the narrative too often meanders, as though Conrad has lost his creative energy. They are backward-looking technically and historically (*The Rover* and *Suspense* dealing with the Napoleonic era), as though Conrad were turning away from the problems of the present and the perennial which he had rendered with such rich intensity in 'Heart of Darkness' and *Nostromo*. In the aftermath of the Great War, literary modernism burgeoned: D. H. Lawrence's *Women in Love* appeared in 1920, Virginia Woolf's *Jacob's Room*, T. S. Eliot's *The Waste Land* and James Joyce's *Ulysses* in 1922. Conrad, who had helped to inaugurate modernism, now seemed to look nostalgically to a bygone world of romance.

The plot and characterization of *The Arrow of Gold* display various signs of regression towards stereotypes: it has an adventurous young hero, a psychically wounded but voluptuously beautiful heroine, a grotesquely melodramatic villain, and an eventual rapturous idyll 'in a small house [. . . .] embowered with roses'. Set in Marseille in the 1870s and dealing with Carlist intrigue, smuggling and sexual rivalry, the novel is partly autobiographical, but the material is predictably romanticized. Conrad had produced the text quite rapidly, largely by dictation, and remarked:

> No colour, no relief, no tonality, the thinnest possible squeaky bubble.

> And when I've finished with it, I shall go out and sell it in a market place for twenty times the money I had for the *Nigger*.

The early reviewers of the book, while endorsing Conrad's eminent reputation, sometimes registered disappointment. 'Here and there in its telling the power of the magician wanes', said John Masefield in the *Times Literary Supplement*; and the guarded praise in the *New Republic* held a warning:

> *The Arrow of Gold* is one of Mr. Conrad's few open-faced novels [. . .] Seldom has his profound knowledge of human nature seemed so little disquieting.

'So little disquieting', indeed. This 'normalization' of Conrad's outlook (a regression towards conventionality in the situations, modes and values of the fiction) has various explanations. One is simply the weariness of an ageing author; another is his acceptance as an eminent figure. It can be seen partly as cause and partly as consequence of his popularity. Knowledge of the appalling sufferings and losses of the Great War strengthened Conrad's tendency to endorse the traditional values of solidarity and stoical heroism, and curbed his tendency to submit those values to the imaginative tests of a corrosive scepticism.

The book of *The Rescue* was published twenty-four years after Conrad had commenced the manuscript. He told Edward Garnett:

> I am settling my affairs in the world and I should not have liked to leave behind me this evidence of having bitten off more than I could chew. A very vulgar vanity.

Of this novel, however it could be said (as has been said of Henry James's later fiction) that its author had chewed more than he had bitten off. The pace of *The Rescue* is heavy and slow, the style is of majestic prolixity; and it develops on a vast scale a sexual thesis that Conrad had more concisely offered long previously, in *Almayer's Folly*: the thesis that sexual passion may incapacitate or 'unman' the man of action, so that he becomes spellbound and betrays his allies. It is as though the weariness of Conrad the ageing writer has infiltrated the muscles of his young hero, Lingard; and the exotic setting – the Java Sea and the jungled shore – resembles an opulently coloured dream. In the *Times Literary Supplement*, Virginia Woolf suggested that 'Mr. Conrad has attempted a romantic theme and in the middle his belief in romance has failed him'. Jocelyn Baines later remarked of *The Rescue*: 'Its mood of defeatism and world-weariness is even more pronounced than that of *Victory*.'

The Rover was the last of Conrad's novels to be completed. Set on the Mediterranean coast of France during the Napoleonic era, it is much less cumbrous, more economical and lucid, than *The Rescue*. Its central character, old Peyrol, retires with his fortune, after many years at sea, to a Provençal farmhouse; eventually, he chooses to help two young lovers by sacrificing his life in a final display of seamanship for a patriotic cause. Of the predominantly enthusiastic response to *The Rover*, Norman Sherry has remarked: 'The critics might well be gushing, but not for reasons that would satisfy Conrad.' *The Times*, for instance, declared that 'everyone will read [*The Rover*] with an enjoyment unmitigated by any necessity for intellectual strivings', while the *Spectator* remarked that it belonged to the category represented by G. A. Henty's historical fiction or R. L. Stevenson's *Treasure Island* – that of the 'adventure novel beloved of boys'. The *New York Times Book Review* frankly noted the novel's 'commercial' veneer. In Britain alone, the first printing numbered 40,000 copies. Swelling international acclaim and burgeoning popularity ensured that at Conrad's death his estate, in spite of his prodigal expenditure, would be worth over £20,000: an ample fortune at that time.

Conrad had hoped in vain to emulate a previous Polish novelist, Henryk Sienkiewicz, by gaining the Nobel Prize for Literature; but he declined other honours: among them, the honorary degrees offered him by the universities of Cambridge, Durham, Edinburgh, Liverpool and Yale, and the knighthood offered in 1924 by Britain's first Labour premier, Ramsay MacDonald. When the sculptor Epstein came to make his bust of the renowned author, he found Conrad 'crippled with rheumatism, crotchety, nervous, and ill. He said to me, "I am finished".' In July 1924 Conrad suffered a heart attack: 'I begin to feel like a cornered rat', he remarked. Another attack followed, on 2 August; and at 8.30 the next morning he fell dead to the floor.

Conrad was buried at Canterbury with Roman Catholic rites. His tombstone bore the words from Spenser's *The Faerie Queene* which he had selected as the epigraph to *The Rover*:

> Sleep after toyle, port after stormie seas,
> Ease after warre, death after life, does greatly please.

In an unintentional irony appropriate to a frequently pessimistic *homo duplex,* those words were originally spoken by the spirit of Despair.

6

Subsequent Reputation

Around the end of Conrad's life there were some significant discordant notes amid the general crescendo of praise. E. M. Forster, reviewing *Notes on Life and Letters,* voiced the complaint (which became famous) that 'the secret casket of his genius contains a vapour rather than a jewel'. Leonard Woolf made much the same point when he remarked of *Suspense*: 'I had the feeling which one gets on cracking a fine, shining, new walnut [. . .] only to find that it has nothing inside it. Most of the later Conrads give one this feeling.' And the *Spectator* said in 1925: 'We begin to see that he was an impressive rather than a likeable writer [. . .] He had stories to tell. And oddly enough he had nothing to say.'

Although such sceptical notes were audible, Conrad's prestige was generally sustained by critics and commentators during the 1920s. G. Jean-Aubry's influential *Joseph Conrad: Life & Letters* appeared in 1927, and there were numerous memoirs of the author, notably those by Jessie Conrad and Ford Madox Ford. By means of the cinema (which Conrad had detested), with its films of *Victory* (1919 and 1930), *Lord Jim* (1925), *Nostromo* (as *The Silver Treasure,* 1926), *Romance* (as *The Road to Romance,* 1927) and *The Rescue* (1929), his fame was reaching a larger audience than he could have imagined possible when he embarked on his literary career. In the 1930s, as later generations of writers (Lawrence, Joyce, Huxley and Auden among them) moved into the foreground of discussion, there was a slackening of interest in him. The novelist Elizabeth Bowen remarked: 'Conrad is in abeyance. We are not clear yet how to rank him; there is an uncertain pause.' Important studies continued to be produced, nevertheless: particularly Gustav Morf's *The Polish Heritage of Joseph Conrad* (1930), Edward Crankshaw's *Joseph Conrad: Some Aspects of the Art of the Novel* (1936) and John Dozier Gordan's *Joseph Conrad: The Making of a Novelist* (1940).

If any single publication marked the end of that 'uncertain pause', it was F. R. Leavis's highly influential *The Great Tradition: George Eliot, Henry James, Joseph Conrad* (1948), which ranked Conrad 'among the very greatest novelists in the language – or any language'. This assessment conveniently coincided with a new 'Collected Edition' published by J. M. Dent, 1946-55. Thereafter the great and still-continuing surge of critical interest swelled, with many of the subsequent commentators taking as their starting-point the bold discriminations made in Leavis's account. Albert Guerard's brilliant critical study, *Conrad the Novelist* (1958), and Jocelyn Baines's fine *Joseph Conrad: A Critical Biography* (1960) were valuable resources. In the wake of modernism, Freudianism, existentialism, the Theatre of the Absurd, and reflecting the age's increasing scepticism about so many beliefs and traditions of the past, critics energetically re-discovered the darker, complex, arcane and sceptical aspects of Conrad's works. Now he seemed less nostalgically romantic and more proleptically subversive. The oblique narrative procedures which had often baffled his contemporaries now seemed largely vindicated by the probing relativism that they implied. The range of approaches burgeoned: for example, there were psychological studies from Thomas Moser and Bernard Meyer; political analyses from Irving Howe, Arnold Kettle, Eloise Knapp Hay and Avrom Fleishman; source-studies by Norman Sherry and Paul Kirschner; analyses of symbolism by Hillis Miller, James Guetti, Donald Yelton, Royal Roussel and Claire Rosenfield. Substantial biographies by Frederick R. Karl and Zdzisław Najder appeared, and Ian Watt's *Conrad in the Nineteenth Century* gave sophisticated accounts of the early works and their background. The United States dominated the field, fulfilling *Nostromo*'s predictions of the USA's economic and cultural hegemony. (In Poland and the USSR, Marxists censored and censured Conrad.)

Of course, after 1945 the vast post-war expansion of higher education in many lands meant that the majority of significant literary figures soon became the centres of expanding industries of research and commentary; but, in the case of Conrad, the scale of the renewed attention was particularly impressive. (The expiry of his copyright in 1974 added new impetus.) In addition to the numerous critical and biographical studies, several lengthy bibliographies appeared; computers produced concordances to a wide range of the novels and tales; Penguin Books and Oxford University

Press ensured the availability of the texts in cheap paperbacks; work proceeded on a scholarly Anglo-American edition of the entire canon; Pléiade in France and Mursia in Italy published new translations; F. R. Karl and Laurence Davies edited numerous volumes of *The Collected Letters*; and Joseph Conrad societies were established in the United States, the United Kingdom, France, Italy, Scandinavia and Poland. Periodicals devoted to the author included *Conradiana* (published in Lubbock, Texas), *Joseph Conrad Today* (Philadelphia and other locations), *The Conradian* (London), *L'Epoque Conradienne* (Limoges), *JCS (Italy) Newsletter* (Pisa) and *The Conrad News* (Gdańsk). Towards the close of the century, the international scale of research mocked the endeavours of bibliographers: excellent scholarly and critical work was being produced not only in the United States and the United Kingdom but also in Scandinavia, continental Europe, Israel, Africa, Japan and elsewhere.

Meanwhile, the cinema industry had continued to exploit Conrad's texts, making films of (among others) *The Secret Agent* (1936), *Under Western Eyes* (1936), *Victory* again (1940), *An Outcast of the Islands* (1952), 'The Secret Sharer' (1952), *Laughing Anne* (1953), *Lord Jim* (1965), *The Rover* (1967), 'The Secret Sharer' again (1973), 'The Duel' (1977) and *An Outcast* again (1979). Orson Welles's masterpiece, *Citizen Kane* (1941), owed its oblique methods partly to Welles's study of *Lord Jim* and 'Heart of Darkness'. Coppola's *Apocalypse Now* (1979) was a spectacular free adaptation of 'Heart of Darkness' which in turn generated *Hearts of Darkness* (1991), a film about the making of the film: it vindicated Conrad's forebodings by its depiction and manifestation of decadence. For television there have been adaptations of *The Shadow-Line*, 'Amy Foster' and *The Secret Agent*. Furthermore, *Under Western Eyes*, *Victory*, 'To-morrow' and *Lord Jim* have been converted into operas by, respectively, John Joubert, Richard Rodney Bennett, Tadeusz Baird and Romuald Twardowski.

Conrad exerted a rich and varied influence on subsequent writers. The paradox of 'the virtue of evil', so vividly expressed in 'Heart of Darkness', was developed further by both T. S. Eliot and Graham Greene. Through the intensity of his corruption, Kurtz gains (intermittently) a stature denied to the mediocre figures around him: perhaps the secular outlook destroys life's significance. In *The Waste Land*, for which this notion provided a theme, Eliot alluded to the tale's opening and had originally chosen as the epigraph a passage culminating in Kurtz's words, 'The horror!' The same theme is pursued in 'The Hollow Men', which not only bears a Conradian title and epigraph but also holds echoes of Marlow's plight when, close to death, he experiences 'some inconceivable world that had no hope in it and no desire'.

Graham Greene's *Brighton Rock* exploits again the paradox of the virtue of evil, as does *The Third Man*, that fine film (in which Kurtz is doubly reincarnated) based on a tale and script by Greene. His greatest debt, however, is probably to *The Secret Agent*; for Greeneland, that seedy, soiled, debased region, has clear affinities with the murky, slimy London of Conrad's novel. There are minor but significant debts: Greene's *It's a Battlefield* borrows an Assistant Commissioner from *The Secret Agent*, and its hero, Conrad Drover, owes his first name to 'a seaman, a merchant officer' who had once lodged in his parents' home. The Conradian theme that loyalty may entail treachery was extensively developed by Greene, as we are reminded by the epigraph, from *Victory*, which heads his novel *The Human Factor*: 'I only know that he who forms a tie is lost. The germ of corruption has entered into his soul.' This theme was present in his early novels (for example, *The Man Within* and *The Name of Action*); and, later, in *A Sort of Life*, he declared that at that period Conrad's influence on him had been 'too great and too disastrous':

> Never again, I swore, would I read a novel of Conrad's – a vow I kept for more than a quarter of a century, until I found myself with *Heart of Darkness* in a small paddle boat travelling up a Congo tributary in 1959 [. . .]

As this passage hints, emulation of the much-travelled Conrad partly accounts for Greene's own adventurous journeys into Africa, America and the East.

Conrad's range is emphasized by the fact that writers as diverse as Virginia Woolf, Malcolm Lowry, John le Carré and V. S. Naipaul have acknowledged his potent presence. As his works, ranging in tone from the lyrical to the satiric, depicted exotic locations and urban squalor, economic imperialism and duplicitous espionage, Conrad provided the bases of many subsequent developments. Woolf's essay 'Modern Fiction' suggested that Conrad's 'Youth' was superior to Joyce's *Ulysses*, and parts of the 'Time Passes' section of *To the Lighthouse* hold echoes of the lyrical-philosophical rhetoric of 'Youth' and the lyrical weatherscapes of *The Mirror of the Sea*. Malcolm Lowry's tribute took the form of a sonnet, 'Joseph Conrad', and commentators have suggested that Lowry's greatest novel, *Under the Volcano,* is variously indebted to 'Heart of Darkness', *Nostromo* and particularly *Lord Jim.* John le Carré's novels of espionage distantly recall *The Secret Agent* and *Under Western Eyes,* and are sprinkled with Conradian allusions. V. S. Naipaul claimed that Conrad 'had been everywhere before me', and reviewers noted that *The Bend in the River* evokes comparisons with 'Heart of Darkness'. In addition, Howard Brenton's televised play of assassination and betrayal, *The Saliva Milkshake,* borrowed its plot largely from the Razumov-Haldin encounter in *Under Western Eyes.*

Continental writers who admired Conrad included André Gide, Thomas Mann and Czesław Miłosz, all of whom paid him handsome tribute. Gide supervised the translation into French of various Conradian works and himself was responsible for the translation of 'Typhoon', while his *Voyage au Congo* is dedicated to Conrad and discusses 'Heart of Darkness'. Mann praised Conrad in *Past Masters and Other Essays,* and Miłosz (in *The Witness of Poetry*) endorsed Mann's view that 'Heart of Darkness' prophetically inaugurated the twentieth century.

In the United States, three major novelists, Ernest Hemingway, Scott Fitzgerald and William Faulkner, were significantly influenced by Conrad. 'From nothing else that I have ever read have I gotten what every book of Conrad has given me', said Hemingway; and connections suggested by critics include the kinship between Conrad's stoical, ageing seamen (Singleton, Whalley, Peyrol) and Hemingway's Santiago (in *The Old Man and the Sea*): an ethic of habitual reticent courage in facing an environment which may be serenely neutral or ruthlessly hostile. Scott Fitzgerald repeatedly extolled Conrad's art, and his intensive study of Conrad's themes and techniques bore fruit in *The Great Gatsby.* Nick Carraway, the partly critical but largely fascinated observer of Gatsby, owes much to Marlow and his ambivalent relationships to Jim and Kurtz. Both writers were fascinated by dreamers and over-reachers, and both saw youth as a time of promise and illusion which dims with experience. Commentators on William Faulkner have postulated various affinities with Conrad: the fondness for multiple narrators, chronological dislocations and the adducing of evidence through imagery as well as event; the interest in absurdity and cruel irony; the interplay of meditative comment and impressionistic starkness; and an ambivalence in treating racial matters. Other American authors who were responsive to Conrad's example include Eugene O'Neill, Jack London, Robert Penn Warren and Herman Wouk.

Several 'Third World' critics, among them Peter Nazareth, D. C. Goonetilleke and C. P. Sarvan, have paid tribute to Conrad's pioneering work as an anti-colonialist author. Nazareth, who explained that he had drawn on *Nostromo* in his own fiction, declared that 'influence' is 'too mild a word for the impact Conrad has had upon the Third World'. Tayeb Salih, of Sudan, acknowledged a Conradian contribution to his *Season of Migration to the North*. The acclaimed novel by Ngugi wa Thiong'o, *A Grain of Wheat* (1967), boldly adapts to Kenyan locations and Kenyan politics various themes and conflicts in *Under Western Eyes*: Haldin and Razumov are relatives of Kihika and Mugo, as Heyst and Lena are relatives of Munira and Wanja in Ngugi's *Petals of Blood*.

In the final quarter of the twentieth century, Conrad's high reputation incurred a number of vigorous challenges. Some Marxist and left-wing critics (notably, Terry Eagleton, Fredric Jameson and Edward Said) postulated his failure to elude the bonds of colonialism. Jameson, for example, alleged in *The Political Unconscious* (1981) that *Nostromo* 'accredits the good opinion the industrial West has of itself' by showing that the South American people, being lazy and shiftless, need to have order imposed on them from abroad. Conrad might have pointed out, in response, a consistent feature of the novels and tales: outsiders who seek to impose order on a foreign region make matters worse and not better. This is true of Lingard's area of Borneo (in *Almayer's Folly* and *An Outcast of the Islands*), of central Africa (as depicted in 'An Outpost of Progress' and 'Heart of Darkness'), of Sumatra's Patusan (in *Lord Jim*), and, according to Mrs Gould and Dr Monygham (supported by the narrator), of Sulaco in *Nostromo*. The text shows that the miners of Sulaco, far from being 'lazy' and 'shiftless', are diligent producers of the state's mineral wealth.

Some black commentators denounced the racism of *The Nigger of the 'Narcissus'* and 'Heart of Darkness'. Chinua Achebe, in particular, initiated a vigorous controversy by alleging that Conrad was 'a bloody racist' who depicted Africa as 'a place of negations [. . .] in comparison with which Europe's own state of spiritual grace will be manifest'. (In response to criticism, Achebe later revised this polemic, changing the notorious phrase from 'a bloody racist' to 'a thoroughgoing racist', and deleting a paragraph which compared Conrad with 'a physician who poisons his patients' and 'those men in Nazi

Germany who lent their talent to the service of virulent racism'.) Other postcolonial writers, including Ngugi wa Thiong'o, Wilson Harris, Frances B. Singh and C. P. Sarvan, argued that though Conrad was certainly ambivalent on racial matters, 'Heart of Darkness' was progressive in its satiric accounts of the colonialists. Sarvan concluded: 'Conrad was not entirely immune to the infection of the beliefs and attitudes of his age, but he was ahead of most in trying to break free.' Singh noted that though 'Heart of Darkness' was now vulnerable in several respects, including the association of Africans with supernatural evil, the story should remain in 'the canon of works indicting colonialism'.

Numerous feminists, including Nina Pelikan Straus, Bette London, Johanna M. Smith and Elaine Showalter, reacted against 'Heart of Darkness', seeing it as both imperialist and sexist. Straus claimed that male critics had repeatedly become accomplices of Marlow, who 'brings truth to men by virtue of his bringing falsehood to women':

> The woman reader [. . .] is in the position to suggest that Marlow's cowardice consists of his inability to face the dangerous self that is the form of his own masculinist vulnerability: his own complicity in the racist, sexist, imperialist, and finally libidinally satisfying world he has shared with Kurtz.

Smith, similarly, alleged that the tale 'reveals the collusion of imperialism and patriarchy: Marlow's narrative aims to "colonize" and pacify both savage darkness and women'. Contrasting voices were heard: Ruth Nadelhaft, for instance, argued that in Conrad's fiction women are centres of intelligent resistance to male vanity and imperialist assumptions: 'Conrad wrote through the critical eyes of women characters.' We may recall that whereas the Marlow of 'Heart of Darkness' said that women should be shielded from the truth, the Marlow of *Chance* says that women know the whole truth but mercifully conceal it from men, who live in a 'fool's paradise'.

These controversies thus extended the arguments broached in Conrad's pages. One of his brilliant achievements was to extend the political range of the English novel by distinctively voicing a coordinated diversity of questions about empire, civilization, race and gender-relationships. By numerous devices, including his mobility of viewpoint and his remarkably free use of the term 'illusion', he suggested that what appears natural, fixed and durable is merely a matter of social convention cemented by habit and guarded by 'a butcher round one corner, a policeman round another'. He thus anticipated a powerful tendency in many recent literary theories: the tendency to proclaim as artificial, as culturally generated and therefore open to change, those areas of belief and identity which once seemed divinely ordained or naturally given and therefore unchangeable. By his power as a questioner, he helped to create the conditions in which his own achievements might be called in question. And by his power as an affirmer – an eloquent affirmer of humane courage, constructive co-operation, and dedication to one's craft – he offers sustenance to readers who enter the tensions and conflicts of the twenty-first century. As he said in 1901:

> The only legitimate basis of creative work lies in the courageous recognition of all the irreconcilable antagonisms that make our life so enigmatic, so burdensome, so fascinating, so dangerous – so full of hope.

Select Bibliography

With a few necessary exceptions, items in the various sections are arranged in chronological order.

BIBLIOGRAPHIES

K. A. Lohf and E. P. Sheehy; *Joseph Conrad at Mid-Century* (Minneapolis: University of Minnesota Press, 1957).

T. G. Ehrsam, *A Bibliography of Joseph Conrad* (Metuchen, NJ: Scarecrow Press, 1969).

B. E. Teets and H. E. Gerber, *Joseph Conrad: An Annotated Bibliography of Writings about Him* (De Kalb, Ill.: Northern Illinois University Press, 1971).

Conradiana magazine frequently publishes bibliographical supplements.

WORKS BY CONRAD (FIRST BRITISH EDITIONS)

Almayer's Folly (London: Fisher Unwin, 1895).

An Outcast of the Islands (London: Fisher Unwin, 1896).

The Nigger of the 'Narcissus' (London: Heinemann, 1897).

Tales of Unrest (London: Fisher Unwin, 1898). Contains 'Karain', 'The Idiots', 'An Outpost of Progress', 'The Return' and 'The Lagoon'.

Lord Jim (Edinburgh and London: Blackwood, 1900).

(With F. M. Hueffer) *The Inheritors* (London: Heinemann, 1901).

Youth: A Narrative/ and Two Other Stories (Edinburgh and London: Blackwood, 1902). Contains 'Youth', 'Heart of Darkness' and 'The End of the Tether'.

Typhoon and Other Stories (London: Heinemann, 1903). Contains 'Typhoon', 'Amy Foster', 'To-morrow' and 'Falk'.

(With Hueffer) *Romance* (London: Smith, Elder, 1903).

Nostromo (London: Harper, 1904).

The Mirror of the Sea (London: Methuen, 1906).
The Secret Agent (London: Methuen, 1907).
A Set of Six (London: Methuen, 1908). Contains 'Gaspar Ruiz', 'The Informer', 'The Brute', 'An Anarchist', 'The Duel' and 'Il Conde'.
Under Western Eyes (London: Methuen, 1911).
Some Reminiscences (London: Nash, 1912). In the USA it was published as *A Personal Record*, the title by which it is generally known today.
'Twixt Land and Sea (London: Dent, 1912). Contains 'A Smile of Fortune', 'The Secret Sharer' and 'Freya of the Seven Isles'.
Chance (London: Methuen, 1914).
Within the Tides (London: Dent, 1915). Contains 'The Planter of Malata', 'The Partner', 'The Inn of the Two Witches' and 'Because of the Dollars'.
Victory (London: Methuen, 1915).
The Shadow-Line (London: Dent, 1917).
The Arrow of Gold (London: Fisher Unwin, 1919).
The Rescue (London: Dent, 1920).
Notes on Life and Letters (London: Dent, 1921).
The Rover (London: Fisher Unwin, 1923).
Tales of Hearsay (London: Fisher Unwin, 1925). Contains 'The Warrior's Soul', 'Prince Roman', 'The Tale' and 'The Black Mate'.
Suspense (London: Dent, 1925)
Last Essays (London: Dent, 1926).

A Note on Editions

The Collected Edition which was published by J. M. Dent & Sons between 1946 and 1955 became, through accessibility and frequent citation, a 'standard' British edition; it was incomplete, however. Cambridge University Press is producing a scholarly edition of the whole canon. Most of Conrad's works are inexpensively available in Penguin and Oxford paperbacks. The Norton editions of selected texts have abundant paraphernalia. Conrad's texts are more diverse than may at first be appreciated: for example, the serial version of *Nostromo* contains important material absent from the first book edition, and that first edition contains important material absent from subsequent editions.

CORRESPONDENCE

Twenty Letters to Joseph Conrad, ed. G. Jean-Aubry (London: First Edition Club, 1926).

Conrad's Polish Background, ed. Zdzisław Najder (London: Oxford University Press, 1964).

Joseph Conrad's Letters to R. B. Cunninghame Graham, ed. C. T. Watts (London: Cambridge University Press, 1969).

The Collected Letters of Joseph Conrad, ed. Frederick R. Karl and Laurence Davies (Cambridge: Cambridge University Press; 1983 onwards).

The editions by Jean-Aubry, Najder and Watts listed above contain material not available in *The Collected Letters*.

BIOGRAPHIES

Jocelyn Baines, *Joseph Conrad: A Critical Biography* (London: Weidenfeld & Nicolson, 1960; repr. Harmondsworth: Penguin, 1971). Lucid and concise, this remains a standard work, though much new material has come to light since the book first appeared.

Bernard C. Meyer, *Joseph Conrad: A Psychoanalytic Biography* (Princeton, NJ: Princeton University Press, 1967). An interesting, though rather reductive, Freudian approach.

Norman Sherry, *Conrad and His World* (London: Thames & Hudson, 1972). A well-illustrated introductory biography.

Frederick R. Karl, *Joseph Conrad: The Three Lives* (New York: Farrar, Straus & Giroux; London: Faber & Faber; 1979). Vast but somewhat speculative.

Ian Watt, *Conrad in the Nineteenth Century* (Berkeley: California University Press, 1979; London: Chatto & Windus, 1980). Gives full, intelligent and sensitive treatment to Conrad's cultural milieu and its influence on the works.

Zdzisław Najder, *Joseph Conrad: A Chronicle* (Cambridge: Cambridge University Press, 1983). A scholarly, well-documented biography.

Cedric Watts, *Joseph Conrad: A Literary Life* (London: Macmillan; New York: St Martin's Press; 1989). A concise account of Conrad's career, emphasizing its economic bases.

Owen Knowles, *A Conrad Chronology* (Boston, Mass.: Hall, 1990). A handy list of biographical facts.

REMINISCENCES

Ford Madox Ford, *Joseph Conrad: A Personal Remembrance* (London: Duckworth, 1924; repr. New York: Octagon Books, 1965). Egoistic, unreliable in details, yet engagingly vivid.

Jessie Conrad, *Joseph Conrad as I Knew Him* (London: Heinemann, 1926). Depicts the difficult (and sometimes dramatic) domestic life.

Borys Conrad, *My Father: Joseph Conrad* (London: Calder & Boyars, 1970); John Conrad, *Joseph Conrad: Times Remembered* (London: Cambridge University Press, 1981). Both sons offer cameos of Joseph Conrad at home and at leisure.

Joseph Conrad: Interviews and Recollections, ed. Martin Ray (London: Macmillan, 1990). An interesting diversity of reminiscences of Conrad.

SCHOLARLY SOURCE-STUDIES

J. D. Gordan, *Conrad: The Making of a Novelist* (Cambridge, Mass.: Harvard University Press, 1940; repr. New York: Russell & Russell, 1963). Discusses the genesis and reception of some early works, particularly *Almayer's Folly, The Nigger* and *Lord Jim*.

Andrzej Busza, 'Conrad's Polish Literary Background': *Antemurale*, 10 (Rome: Institutum Historicum Polonicum, 1966). Suggests connections between numerous Polish texts and Conrad's literary works.

Norman Sherry, *Conrad's Eastern World* (London: Cambridge University Press, 1966). Adduces factual source-materials of Conrad's 'eastern' fiction.

Paul Kirschner, *Conrad: The Psychologist as Artist* (Edinburgh: Oliver & Boyd, 1968). The latter part of this book illustrates Conrad's indebtedness to French authors, particularly Maupassant and Anatole France.

Norman Sherry, *Conrad's Western World* (London: Cambridge University Press, 1971). Cites factual sources of 'Heart of Darkness', *Nostromo* and *The Secret Agent*.

CRITICISM

Numerous early reviews of Conrad's works are gathered in *Conrad: The Critical Heritage*, ed. Norman Sherry (London: Routledge & Kegan Paul, 1973), and in *Joseph Conrad: Critical Assessments*, ed. Keith Carabine, vol. I (Mountfield: Helm Information, 1992).

Max Beerbohm, '"The Feast" by J-s-ph C-nr-d', in *A Christmas Garland* (London: Heinemann, 1912; reprinted in volume I of *Joseph Conrad: Critical Assessments*). A brilliant parody of the techniques and sceptical ideas in Conrad's earlier works. ('Within the hut the form of the white man, corpulent and pale, was covered with a mosquito-net that was itself illusory like everything else, only more so.')

F. R. Leavis, *The Great Tradition* (London: Chatto & Windus, 1948; repr. Harmondsworth: Penguin, 1962; repr. New York: New York University Press, 1963). A highly influential discussion.

Douglas Hewitt, *Conrad: A Reassessment* (Cambridge: Bowes & Bowes, 1952; revised edn.: London: Bowes & Bowes, 1975). Incisive critical judgements, often shrewder than Leavis's.

Thomas Moser, *Joseph Conrad: Achievement and Decline* (Cambridge, Mass.: Harvard University Press, 1957; repr. Hamden, Conn.: Archon Books, 1966). An influential survey, relating Conrad's decline to the 'uncongenial' topic of sexual love.

Albert Guerard, *Conrad the Novelist* (Cambridge, Mass.: Harvard University Press, 1958; repr. New York: Athenaeum, 1967). At times too Jungian, but usually vigorous, subtle and suggestive.

The Art of Joseph Conrad: A Critical Symposium, ed. R. W. Stallman (East Lansing: Michigan State University Press, 1960). Includes valuable material by André Gide, Ramón Fernández, Czesław Miłosz and others.

Eloise Knapp Hay, *The Political Novels of Joseph Conrad* (Chicago and London: Chicago University Press, 1963). Emphasizes the humanely liberal aspects of Conrad's political outlook.

Avrom Fleishman, *Conrad's Politics* (Baltimore: Johns Hopkins, 1967). Locates Conrad in an 'organicist' tradition.

F. R. Leavis, *'Anna Karenina' and Other Essays* (London: Chatto & Windus, 1967). Includes essays on *The Shadow-Line* and 'The Secret Sharer'.

Terry Eagleton, *Exiles and Emigrés* (London: Chatto & Windus, 1970). Contains a perceptive discussion of *Under Western Eyes*.

Chinua Achebe, 'An Image of Africa' (lecture given in 1975), *The Chancellor Lecture Series 1974-5* (Amherst: University of Massachusetts, 1976), reprinted in *Massachusetts Review*, 18 (Autumn 1977). A denunciation of Conrad as 'a bloody racist'. Achebe moderated his criticism when revising the piece: see 'An Image of Africa' in *Heart of Darkness*, ed. Robert Kimbrough (3rd edn.: New York: Norton, 1988), where it is followed by responses by Wilson Harris, Frances B. Singh and C. P. Sarvan.

Terry Eagleton, *Criticism and Ideology* (London: NLB, 1976). A Marxist account which (in a chapter described by Eagleton as 'partial and reductive') depicts Conrad as 'deadlocked', trapped in ideological self-contradiction.

Cedric Watts, *Conrad's 'Heart of Darkness': A Critical and Contextual Discussion* (Milan: Mursia, 1977). Approaches this novella from numerous angles.

J. A. Verleun, *The Stone Horse* (Groningen: Bouma's Boekhuis, 1978). A scrupulous analysis of parts of *Nostromo*.

Jacques Berthoud, *Joseph Conrad: The Major Phase* (London: Cambridge University Press, 1978). Thoughtful discussions of the major works.

Cedric Watts, *A Preface to Conrad* (London and New York: Longman, 1982; 2nd edn.: Longman, 1993). An introductory survey of texts and contexts.

Fredric Jameson, *The Political Unconscious: Narrative as a Socially Symbolic Act* (London: Methuen, 1981). Includes an influential but rather reductive account of Conrad.

Cedric Watts, *The Deceptive Text: An Introduction to Covert Plots* (Brighton: Harvester; Totowa, NJ: Barnes & Noble, 1984). Shows how numerous works, by Conrad and other writers, incorporate concealed plot-sequences.

Robert Secor and Debra Moddelmog, *Joseph Conrad and American Writers* (Westport, Conn.; London: Greenwood Press, 1985). Suggests a range of possible influences.

The Ugo Mursia Memorial Lectures, ed. Mario Curreli (Milan: Mursia, 1988). This tribute to a leading Italian Conradian provides an international diversity of approaches.

Jakob Lothe, *Conrad's Narrative Method* (Oxford: Oxford University Press, 1989). A painstakingly judicious analysis of narrative techniques.

Joseph Conrad: 'Heart of Darkness': A Case Study in Contemporary Criticism, ed. Ross C. Murfin (New York: St Martin's Press, 1989). This includes a vigorous feminist essay by Johanna M. Smith: '"Too Beautiful Altogether": Patriarchal Ideology in *Heart of Darkness*'.

Jeremy Hawthorn, *Joseph Conrad: Narrative Technique and Ideological Commitment* (London: Arnold, 1990). Discusses various relationships between morality and technique.

Bette London, *The Appropriated Voice: Narrative Authority in Conrad, Forster, and Woolf* (Ann Arbor: Michigan University Press, 1990). Vehemently discredits Conrad by claiming that 'Marlow virulently discredits the world of women'.

Daphna Erdinast-Vulcan, *Joseph Conrad and the Modern Temper* (Oxford: Oxford University Press, 1991). Depicts Conrad as 'an incurable moralist infected with the ethical relativism of his age'.

Elaine Showalter, *Sexual Anarchy* (London: Bloomsbury, 1991). Claims that 'Heart of Darkness' explicitly and implicitly excludes females from knowledge of reality.

Ruth Nadelhaft, *Joseph Conrad* (Hemel Hempstead: Harvester Wheatsheaf, 1991). Argues that Conrad depicts women as centres of resistance to male vanity and imperialist assumptions.

Joseph Conrad: Critical Assessments (4 volumes), ed. Keith Carabine (Mountfield: Helm Information, 1992). Though there are editorial lapses, this vast compendium of previously published material (mainly from magazines) is a rich resource.

BACKGROUND READING

Arthur Schopenhauer, *The World as Will and Idea* (1818; London: Routledge & Kegan Paul, 1957). A major source of the pessimistic ideas in Conrad's early works.

Adam Mickiewicz, *Pan Tadeusz* (written around 1832–4), trans. G. R. Noyes (London: Dent, 1930). The fine Polish epic which provided themes and techniques for Conradian development.

Other nineteenth-century writers who influenced Conrad were Dickens, Turgenev, Flaubert, Dostoevsky, Anatole France (whose long life extended well into the twentieth century), Maupassant and Stephen Crane.

Viktor Shklovsky, 'Art as Technique' (1917), in *Russian Formalist Criticism*, ed. L. T. Lemon and M. J. Reis (Lincoln, Neb.: University of Nebraska Press, 1965). This theory of 'defamiliarization' does not cite Conrad but is usefully applicable to his work.

Terry Eagleton, *Literary Theory* (Oxford: Blackwell, 1983). A lively introduction to the theories which burgeoned in the period 1950-80 and which had sometimes been anticipated critically by Conrad.

Alistair Fowler, *A History of English Literature* (Oxford: Blackwell, 1987). A good panoramic survey.

Index

(Works are listed after their authors' names.)

WRITERS AND THEIR WORK

"... this series promises to outshine its own obviously high reputation."
Times Higher Education Supplement

"... will build into a fine multi-volume critical encyclopaedia of English literature."
Library Review & Reference Review

"... Excellent, informative, readable, and recommended."
NATE News

"written by outstanding contemporary critics, whose expertise is flavoured by unashamed enthusiasm for their subjects and the series' diverse aspirations."
Times Educational Supplement

"A useful and timely addition to the ranks of the lit crit and reviews genre. Written in an accessible and authoritative style."
Library Association Record

WRITERS AND THEIR WORK

Title	Author
Alfred Tennyson	*Seamus Perry*
Anita Desai	*Elaine Yee Lin Ho*
Anthony Trollope	*Andrew Sanders*
Byron	*Drummond Bone*
C.S. Lewis	*William Gray*
Charles Dickens	*Rod Mengham*
Chinua Achebe	*Nahem Yousaf*
D.H. Lawrence	*Linda Ruth Williams*
E.M. Forster	*Nicholas Royle*
Franz Kafka	*Michael Wood*
George Eliot	*Josephine McDonagh*
George Orwell	*Douglas Kerr*
Gerard Manley Hopkins	*Daniel Brown*
Harold Pinter	*Mark Taylor-Batty*
Henrik Ibsen, 2nd edition	*Sally Ledger*
Henry James—The Later Writing	*Barbara Hardy*
Jane Austen	*Robert Miles*
John Keats	*Kelvin Everest*
Joseph Conrad	*Cedric Watts*
Leo Tolstoy	*John Bayley*
Oscar Wilde	*Alexandra Warwick*
Paul Scott	*Jacqueline Banerjee*
Percy Bysshe Shelley	*Paul Hamilton*
Philip Larkin, 2nd Edition	*Laurence Lerner*
Robert Browning	*John Woolford*
Rudyard Kipling	*Jan Montefiore*
Samuel Beckett	*Sinéad Mooney*

WRITERS AND THEIR WORK

Title	Author
Samuel Taylor Coleridge	*Stephen Bygrave*
Shashi Deshpande	*Amrita Bhalla*
Sir Walter Scott	*Harriet Harvey Wood*
Stephen Crane	*Kevin J. Hayes*
Swinburne	*Catherine Maxwell*
Sylvia Plath, 2nd edition	*Elisabeth Bronfen*
T.S. Eliot	*Colin MacCabe*
Ted Hughes	*Susan Bassnett*
Thomas Hardy, 2nd Edition	*Peter Widdowson*
V.S. Naipaul	*Suman Gupta*
Victorian Quest Romance	*Robert Fraser*
Virginia Woolf, 2nd Edition	*Laura Marcus*
W.B. Yeasts	*Edward Larrissy*
William Blake	*Steve Vine*
William Golding, 2nd Edition	*Kevin McCarron*
William Makepeace Thackeray	*Richard Salmon*
Wole Soyinka	*Mpalive-Hangson Msiska*